100 Slow Cooking Recipes for Home

By: Kelly Johnson

Table of Contents

Soups and Stews:
- Slow Cooker Chicken Noodle Soup
- Beef and Vegetable Stew
- Vegetarian Chili
- Lentil Soup
- Chicken Tortilla Soup
- Split Pea Soup
- Butternut Squash Soup
- White Bean and Kale Soup
- Potato Leek Soup
- Slow Cooker Minestrone

Meaty Delights:
- Slow Cooker Pulled Pork
- BBQ Ribs
- Beef Stroganoff
- Honey Garlic Chicken
- Italian Meatballs
- Slow Cooker Pot Roast
- Lemon Herb Chicken
- Sausage and Peppers
- Teriyaki Pork Tenderloin
- Cuban Mojo Pork
- Pork Carnitas
- Barbecue Beef Brisket
- Slow Cooker Lamb Curry
- Beer-Braised Pot Roast
- Asian Pulled Pork Tacos

Vegetarian Delights:
- Eggplant Parmesan
- Vegetarian Bolognese
- Crockpot Ratatouille
- Slow Cooker Mac and Cheese
- Quinoa and Vegetable Stew
- Vegetarian Gumbo
- Mexican Quinoa Casserole
- Slow Cooker Enchiladas
- Vegetarian Tikka Masala

Soups and Stews:

- Vegetable Lasagna
- Vegan Butternut Squash Curry
- Slow Cooker Eggplant Lasagna
- Chickpea and Vegetable Curry
- Slow Cooker Sweet Potato and Quinoa Stew
- Vegan Lentil Sloppy Joes
- Slow Cooker Ratatouille
- Vegan Black Bean and Pumpkin Chili
- Slow Cooker Cauliflower Curry
- Vegetarian Cabbage Rolls
- Vegan Moroccan Chickpea Tagine

- Slow Cooker Apple Crisp
- Chocolate Lava Cake
- Slow Cooker Rice Pudding
- Peach Cobbler
- Caramelized Bananas
- Slow Cooker Bread Pudding
- Chocolate Fondue
- Berry Compote
- Slow Cooker Tiramisu
- Pumpkin Spice Latte

Chicken Creations:

- Chicken Curry
- Lemon Garlic Chicken Thighs
- Buffalo Chicken Dip
- Chicken Alfredo Pasta
- Honey Mustard Chicken
- Coq au Vin
- Chicken and Dumplings
- Chicken Fajitas
- Lemon Herb Chicken and Potatoes
- Chicken Tikka Masala
- Balsamic Glazed CHicken
- Slow Cooker Chicken Marsala
- Greek Chicken Gyros
- Cranberry Orange Chicken
- Cajun Chicken and Sausage Jambalaya

Hearty Soups and Chilis:

- Black Bean Soup
- Tuscan White Bean Soup

- Mexican Chicken Tortilla Chili
- Slow Cooker Lentil Chili
- Moroccan Chickpea Stew
- Ham and Bean Soup
- Slow Cooker Sausage and Lentil Stew
- Vegetarian Taco Soup
- Wild Rice and Mushroom Soup
- Thai Coconut Chicken Soup

Sides and Dips:

- Creamy Slow Cooker Mashed Potatoes
- Slow Cooker Baked Beans
- Caramelized Onion Dip
- Artichoke and Spinach Dip
- Slow Cooker Risotto
- Garlic Parmesan Bread Pudding
- Buffalo Chicken Dip
- Slow Cooker Cornbread
- Jalapeño Popper Dip
- Slow Cooker Rosemary Garlic Potatoes

Soups and Stews:
Slow Cooker Chicken Noodle Soup

Ingredients:

- 1 pound boneless, skinless chicken breasts or thighs
- 8 cups chicken broth
- 3 carrots, sliced
- 3 celery stalks, sliced
- 1 onion, diced
- 3 cloves garlic, minced
- 1 teaspoon dried thyme
- 1 teaspoon dried rosemary
- 1 bay leaf
- Salt and pepper to taste
- 2 cups egg noodles (or any pasta of your choice)
- Fresh parsley, chopped, for garnish

Instructions:

Prepare Ingredients:
- Place the chicken breasts or thighs in the slow cooker. Add sliced carrots, sliced celery, diced onion, minced garlic, dried thyme, dried rosemary, bay leaf, salt, and pepper.

Add Chicken Broth:
- Pour the chicken broth over the ingredients in the slow cooker. Make sure the broth covers the chicken and vegetables.

Cook on Low:
- Cover and cook on low for 6-8 hours or until the chicken is cooked through and vegetables are tender.

Shred Chicken:
- About 30 minutes before serving, remove the chicken from the slow cooker and shred it using two forks. Return the shredded chicken to the slow cooker.

Add Noodles:
- Add the egg noodles (or pasta of your choice) to the slow cooker. Cook for an additional 15-20 minutes or until the noodles are tender.

Adjust Seasoning:

- Taste the soup and adjust the seasoning with salt and pepper as needed. Remove the bay leaf.

Garnish and Serve:
- Ladle the soup into bowls, garnish with chopped fresh parsley, and serve hot.

This Slow Cooker Chicken Noodle Soup is a comforting and classic dish that's easy to prepare. The slow cooking process allows the flavors to meld, creating a delicious and hearty soup. Enjoy this warm and satisfying meal, especially on chilly days or when you're feeling under the weather!

Beef and Vegetable Stew

Ingredients:

- 2 pounds beef stew meat, cut into bite-sized pieces
- 1/4 cup all-purpose flour
- Salt and pepper to taste
- 2 tablespoons olive oil
- 1 onion, chopped
- 3 cloves garlic, minced
- 4 cups beef broth
- 1 cup red wine (optional)
- 2 tablespoons tomato paste
- 1 teaspoon dried thyme
- 1 teaspoon dried rosemary
- 3 carrots, peeled and sliced
- 3 celery stalks, sliced
- 3 potatoes, peeled and diced
- 1 cup frozen peas
- 1 cup frozen green beans
- Fresh parsley, chopped, for garnish

Instructions:

Coat Beef with Flour:
- In a large bowl, toss the beef stew meat with flour, salt, and pepper until the meat is coated.

Brown Beef:
- In a large skillet, heat olive oil over medium-high heat. Add the coated beef pieces and brown on all sides. Transfer the browned beef to the slow cooker.

Sauté Onion and Garlic:
- In the same skillet, add chopped onion and minced garlic. Sauté until the onion is translucent, scraping up any browned bits from the bottom of the skillet. Transfer the onion and garlic to the slow cooker.

Add Liquids and Tomato Paste:
- Pour beef broth, red wine (if using), and tomato paste into the slow cooker. Add dried thyme and dried rosemary. Stir to combine.

Cook on Low:
- Cover and cook on low for 7-8 hours or until the beef is tender.

Add Vegetables:
- About 30 minutes before serving, add sliced carrots, sliced celery, diced potatoes, frozen peas, and frozen green beans to the slow cooker. Stir to combine.

Adjust Seasoning:
- Taste the stew and adjust the seasoning with salt and pepper if needed.

Serve:
- Ladle the Beef and Vegetable Stew into bowls, garnish with chopped fresh parsley, and serve hot.

This slow cooker beef and vegetable stew is a comforting and nutritious meal that's perfect for a cozy dinner. The slow cooking process allows the flavors to meld together, resulting in a rich and flavorful stew. Enjoy!

Vegetarian Chili

Ingredients:

- 2 cans (15 oz each) black beans, drained and rinsed
- 2 cans (15 oz each) kidney beans, drained and rinsed
- 1 can (15 oz) chickpeas, drained and rinsed
- 1 large onion, diced
- 3 cloves garlic, minced
- 1 bell pepper, diced (any color)
- 1 zucchini, diced
- 1 cup corn kernels (fresh or frozen)
- 1 can (28 oz) diced tomatoes, undrained
- 1 can (15 oz) tomato sauce
- 1 cup vegetable broth
- 2 tablespoons chili powder
- 1 tablespoon ground cumin
- 1 teaspoon paprika
- 1 teaspoon dried oregano
- 1/2 teaspoon cayenne pepper (optional, for heat)
- Salt and black pepper to taste
- 1 cup shredded cheddar cheese (for serving, optional)
- Sour cream or Greek yogurt (for serving, optional)
- Fresh cilantro, chopped (for garnish, optional)
- Green onions, chopped (for garnish, optional)
- Tortilla chips (for serving, optional)

Instructions:

Combine Ingredients in Slow Cooker:
- In the slow cooker, combine black beans, kidney beans, chickpeas, diced onion, minced garlic, diced bell pepper, diced zucchini, corn kernels, diced tomatoes, tomato sauce, and vegetable broth.

Season the Chili:
- Add chili powder, ground cumin, paprika, dried oregano, cayenne pepper (if using), salt, and black pepper. Stir well to combine.

Cook on Low:
- Cover and cook on low for 6-8 hours or until the vegetables are tender and the flavors meld together.

Adjust Seasoning:
- Taste the chili and adjust the seasoning if needed, adding more salt or spices to your liking.

Serve:
- Ladle the Vegetarian Chili into bowls. Optionally, top with shredded cheddar cheese, a dollop of sour cream or Greek yogurt, fresh cilantro, green onions, and serve with tortilla chips on the side.

This Vegetarian Chili is not only hearty and satisfying but also packed with nutritious ingredients. The slow cooking process allows the flavors to develop, making it a delicious and comforting meal. Enjoy!

Lentil Soup

Ingredients:

- 1 cup dried green or brown lentils, rinsed and drained
- 1 onion, diced
- 3 carrots, peeled and sliced
- 3 celery stalks, sliced
- 3 cloves garlic, minced
- 1 can (14 oz) diced tomatoes, undrained
- 6 cups vegetable broth
- 1 teaspoon ground cumin
- 1 teaspoon ground coriander
- 1 teaspoon smoked paprika
- 1/2 teaspoon ground turmeric
- 1 bay leaf
- Salt and black pepper to taste
- 3 cups fresh spinach or kale, chopped
- Fresh lemon juice (optional, for serving)
- Fresh parsley, chopped (for garnish, optional)

Instructions:

Combine Ingredients in Slow Cooker:
- In the slow cooker, combine lentils, diced onion, sliced carrots, sliced celery, minced garlic, diced tomatoes, vegetable broth, ground cumin, ground coriander, smoked paprika, ground turmeric, bay leaf, salt, and black pepper.

Cook on Low:
- Cover and cook on low for 6-8 hours or until lentils are tender.

Add Greens:
- About 30 minutes before serving, stir in the chopped spinach or kale. Adjust seasoning if needed.

Remove Bay Leaf:
- Discard the bay leaf before serving.

Serve:
- Ladle the Lentil Soup into bowls. Optionally, squeeze fresh lemon juice on top and garnish with chopped fresh parsley.

This Slow Cooker Lentil Soup is a nutritious and satisfying dish that's easy to prepare. The slow cooking allows the lentils to become tender and absorb the flavors of the vegetables and spices. Enjoy this comforting soup for a wholesome meal!

Chicken Tortilla Soup

Ingredients:

- 1 pound boneless, skinless chicken breasts
- 1 can (15 oz) black beans, drained and rinsed
- 1 can (15 oz) diced tomatoes, undrained
- 1 cup frozen corn kernels
- 1 onion, diced
- 3 cloves garlic, minced
- 1 jalapeño, seeds removed and diced (optional, for heat)
- 1 red bell pepper, diced
- 1 teaspoon ground cumin
- 1 teaspoon chili powder
- 1/2 teaspoon paprika
- 1/2 teaspoon dried oregano
- 4 cups chicken broth
- Salt and black pepper to taste
- Juice of 1 lime
- 1/4 cup fresh cilantro, chopped
- Tortilla strips or chips (for serving)
- Avocado slices (for serving)
- Shredded cheese (cheddar or Mexican blend, for serving)
- Sour cream (for serving)

Instructions:

Place Ingredients in Slow Cooker:
- In the slow cooker, combine chicken breasts, black beans, diced tomatoes, frozen corn, diced onion, minced garlic, diced jalapeño (if using), diced red bell pepper, ground cumin, chili powder, paprika, dried oregano, chicken broth, salt, and black pepper.

Cook on Low:
- Cover and cook on low for 6-8 hours or until the chicken is cooked through and easily shreddable.

Shred Chicken:
- Remove the chicken breasts from the slow cooker and shred using two forks. Return the shredded chicken to the soup.

Add Lime Juice and Cilantro:

- Stir in the lime juice and chopped cilantro. Adjust seasoning if needed.

Serve:
- Ladle the Chicken Tortilla Soup into bowls. Top with tortilla strips or chips, avocado slices, shredded cheese, and a dollop of sour cream.

This Slow Cooker Chicken Tortilla Soup is a flavorful and comforting dish with a hint of spice. The combination of tender chicken, beans, and vibrant vegetables creates a satisfying soup that's perfect for any time of the year. Enjoy!

Split Pea Soup

Ingredients:

- 2 cups dried green split peas, rinsed and drained
- 1 ham hock or 1 cup diced ham
- 1 onion, diced
- 3 carrots, peeled and sliced
- 3 celery stalks, sliced
- 3 cloves garlic, minced
- 1 bay leaf
- 8 cups vegetable or chicken broth
- Salt and black pepper to taste
- 1 teaspoon dried thyme
- 1 teaspoon dried marjoram
- 1 tablespoon olive oil
- 2 cups potatoes, peeled and diced
- Fresh parsley, chopped (for garnish, optional)

Instructions:

Combine Ingredients in Slow Cooker:
- In the slow cooker, combine split peas, ham hock or diced ham, diced onion, sliced carrots, sliced celery, minced garlic, bay leaf, broth, salt, black pepper, dried thyme, and dried marjoram.

Cook on Low:
- Cover and cook on low for 6-8 hours or until the split peas are tender.

Sauté Potatoes:
- In a skillet, heat olive oil over medium heat. Sauté the diced potatoes until they are lightly browned on the edges.

Add Potatoes to Soup:
- About 30 minutes before serving, add the sautéed potatoes to the slow cooker. Stir to combine.

Remove Ham Hock and Bay Leaf:
- If using a ham hock, remove it from the slow cooker. Shred any meat and add it back to the soup. Discard the bay leaf.

Adjust Seasoning:
- Taste the soup and adjust the seasoning with salt and pepper if needed.

Serve:
- Ladle the Split Pea Soup into bowls. Garnish with chopped fresh parsley if desired.

This Slow Cooker Split Pea Soup is a classic and comforting dish. The slow cooking process allows the flavors to meld, creating a rich and hearty soup. Enjoy the warmth and nourishment of this delicious bowl!

Butternut Squash Soup

Ingredients:

- 1 large butternut squash, peeled, seeded, and diced
- 1 onion, diced
- 2 carrots, peeled and sliced
- 2 apples, peeled, cored, and diced
- 3 cloves garlic, minced
- 4 cups vegetable broth
- 1 teaspoon ground cinnamon
- 1/2 teaspoon ground nutmeg
- 1/2 teaspoon ground ginger
- 1/2 teaspoon dried thyme
- Salt and black pepper to taste
- 1 cup coconut milk or heavy cream
- 2 tablespoons maple syrup (optional, for sweetness)
- Chopped fresh parsley or chives (for garnish, optional)

Instructions:

Combine Ingredients in Slow Cooker:
- In the slow cooker, combine diced butternut squash, diced onion, sliced carrots, diced apples, minced garlic, vegetable broth, ground cinnamon, ground nutmeg, ground ginger, dried thyme, salt, and black pepper.

Cook on Low:
- Cover and cook on low for 6-8 hours or until the vegetables are tender.

Blend the Soup:
- Use an immersion blender or transfer the soup in batches to a blender. Blend until smooth and creamy.

Add Coconut Milk and Maple Syrup:
- Stir in the coconut milk or heavy cream and maple syrup (if using). Adjust seasoning if needed.

Serve:
- Ladle the Butternut Squash Soup into bowls. Garnish with chopped fresh parsley or chives if desired.

This Slow Cooker Butternut Squash Soup is velvety, flavorful, and perfect for cooler days. The combination of butternut squash, apples, and warming spices creates a comforting soup. Enjoy the richness and sweetness of this delightful dish!

White Bean and Kale Soup

Ingredients:

- 2 cans (15 oz each) white beans, drained and rinsed
- 1 onion, diced
- 3 carrots, peeled and sliced
- 3 celery stalks, sliced
- 3 cloves garlic, minced
- 1 teaspoon dried rosemary
- 1 teaspoon dried thyme
- 1 bay leaf
- 4 cups vegetable broth
- 1 can (14 oz) diced tomatoes, undrained
- 1 bunch kale, stems removed and leaves chopped
- Salt and black pepper to taste
- 1 tablespoon olive oil
- 1 tablespoon lemon juice
- Grated Parmesan cheese (for serving, optional)

Instructions:

Combine Ingredients in Slow Cooker:
- In the slow cooker, combine white beans, diced onion, sliced carrots, sliced celery, minced garlic, dried rosemary, dried thyme, bay leaf, vegetable broth, diced tomatoes, and chopped kale.

Cook on Low:
- Cover and cook on low for 6-8 hours or until the vegetables are tender.

Sauté Kale:
- In a skillet, heat olive oil over medium heat. Add the chopped kale and sauté for a few minutes until wilted.

Add Sautéed Kale:
- About 30 minutes before serving, add the sautéed kale to the slow cooker. Stir to combine.

Remove Bay Leaf:
- Discard the bay leaf before serving.

Season and Serve:

- Season the soup with salt, black pepper, and lemon juice to taste. Ladle the White Bean and Kale Soup into bowls. Optionally, top with grated Parmesan cheese.

This Slow Cooker White Bean and Kale Soup is a nutritious and flavorful dish that's easy to prepare. The combination of white beans, hearty vegetables, and kale creates a satisfying and wholesome meal. Enjoy the warmth and goodness of this delicious soup!

Potato Leek Soup

Ingredients:

- 4 large leeks, white and light green parts, sliced
- 4 large potatoes, peeled and diced
- 1 onion, diced
- 3 cloves garlic, minced
- 4 cups vegetable or chicken broth
- 1 teaspoon dried thyme
- 1 bay leaf
- Salt and black pepper to taste
- 4 cups water
- 1 cup whole milk or heavy cream
- Chopped fresh chives (for garnish, optional)

Instructions:

Combine Ingredients in Slow Cooker:
- In the slow cooker, combine sliced leeks, diced potatoes, diced onion, minced garlic, vegetable or chicken broth, dried thyme, bay leaf, salt, and black pepper.

Cook on Low:
- Cover and cook on low for 6-8 hours or until the potatoes are tender.

Blend Soup:
- Use an immersion blender to blend the soup until smooth. If you don't have an immersion blender, carefully transfer the soup in batches to a blender and blend until smooth.

Add Water and Milk or Cream:
- Stir in water and milk or cream. Adjust the consistency to your liking by adding more water if needed. Remove the bay leaf.

Season and Serve:
- Season the Potato Leek Soup with additional salt and black pepper if needed. Ladle the soup into bowls. Optionally, garnish with chopped fresh chives.

This Slow Cooker Potato Leek Soup is creamy, flavorful, and perfect for a comforting meal. The slow cooking allows the flavors to meld, creating a rich and satisfying soup. Enjoy the warmth of this classic dish!

Slow Cooker Minestrone

Ingredients:

- 1 can (15 oz) kidney beans, drained and rinsed
- 1 can (15 oz) cannellini beans, drained and rinsed
- 1 cup chopped zucchini
- 1 cup chopped carrots
- 1 cup chopped celery
- 1 onion, diced
- 3 cloves garlic, minced
- 1 can (14 oz) diced tomatoes, undrained
- 1 can (6 oz) tomato paste
- 6 cups vegetable broth
- 1 teaspoon dried oregano
- 1 teaspoon dried basil
- 1/2 teaspoon dried thyme
- Salt and black pepper to taste
- 1 cup small pasta (such as ditalini or small shells)
- 2 cups chopped spinach or kale
- 1/2 cup grated Parmesan cheese (for serving, optional)
- Fresh basil, chopped (for garnish, optional)

Instructions:

Combine Ingredients in Slow Cooker:
- In the slow cooker, combine kidney beans, cannellini beans, chopped zucchini, chopped carrots, chopped celery, diced onion, minced garlic, diced tomatoes, tomato paste, vegetable broth, dried oregano, dried basil, dried thyme, salt, and black pepper.

Cook on Low:
- Cover and cook on low for 6-8 hours or until the vegetables are tender.

Add Pasta:
- About 30 minutes before serving, add the small pasta to the slow cooker. Stir to combine.

Add Spinach or Kale:
- About 10 minutes before serving, stir in the chopped spinach or kale. Adjust seasoning if needed.

Serve:
- Ladle the Minestrone Soup into bowls. Optionally, top with grated Parmesan cheese and chopped fresh basil.

This Slow Cooker Minestrone Soup is a hearty and nutritious dish with a variety of vegetables and beans. The slow cooking allows the flavors to meld, creating a comforting and flavorful soup. Enjoy this classic Italian soup on a chilly day!

Meaty Delights:
Slow Cooker Pulled Pork

Ingredients:

- 3-4 pounds pork shoulder or pork butt
- 1 tablespoon brown sugar
- 1 tablespoon paprika
- 1 tablespoon garlic powder
- 1 tablespoon onion powder
- 1 teaspoon cayenne pepper (adjust to taste)
- 1 teaspoon ground cumin
- 1 teaspoon dried thyme
- Salt and black pepper to taste
- 1 cup chicken broth or apple juice
- 1/4 cup apple cider vinegar
- 1/4 cup Worcestershire sauce
- 1/4 cup soy sauce
- 1/4 cup ketchup
- 1/4 cup brown sugar (for sauce)
- 1/4 cup apple cider vinegar (for sauce)
- Hamburger buns, for serving
- Coleslaw, for topping (optional)

Instructions:

Prepare the Pork:
- Trim excess fat from the pork shoulder or pork butt. In a small bowl, mix together brown sugar, paprika, garlic powder, onion powder, cayenne pepper, ground cumin, dried thyme, salt, and black pepper to create a dry rub. Rub the mixture evenly over the pork.

Place in Slow Cooker:
- Place the seasoned pork in the slow cooker.

Prepare Liquid Mixture:
- In a separate bowl, mix together chicken broth or apple juice, 1/4 cup apple cider vinegar, Worcestershire sauce, soy sauce, ketchup, 1/4 cup brown sugar, and 1/4 cup apple cider vinegar.

Cook on Low:

- Pour the liquid mixture over the pork in the slow cooker. Cover and cook on low for 8 hours or until the pork is fork-tender and easily shreddable.

Shred the Pork:
- Once cooked, remove the pork from the slow cooker and shred it using two forks. Remove any excess fat.

Prepare Sauce:
- Strain the liquid from the slow cooker and transfer it to a saucepan. Bring to a simmer and let it reduce until slightly thickened.

Combine Pork and Sauce:
- Mix the shredded pork with the reduced sauce. Adjust seasoning if needed.

Serve:
- Serve the pulled pork on hamburger buns. Optionally, top with coleslaw for added freshness.

This Slow Cooker Pulled Pork is flavorful, tender, and perfect for sandwiches. The slow cooking process allows the pork to absorb the delicious flavors. Enjoy this classic comfort food with your favorite sides!

BBQ Ribs

Ingredients:

- 2 racks of baby back ribs
- Salt and black pepper to taste
- 1 tablespoon garlic powder
- 1 tablespoon onion powder
- 1 tablespoon smoked paprika
- 1 teaspoon cayenne pepper (adjust to taste)
- 1 cup BBQ sauce (plus extra for serving)
- 1/2 cup apple cider vinegar
- 1/4 cup brown sugar
- 2 tablespoons Dijon mustard

Instructions:

Prepare the Ribs:
- Remove the membrane from the back of the ribs for tenderness. Season the ribs with salt, black pepper, garlic powder, onion powder, smoked paprika, and cayenne pepper.

Cut and Arrange in Slow Cooker:
- Cut the racks of ribs into sections that will fit in your slow cooker. Stand the sections along the inside edge of the slow cooker, with the meaty side facing out.

Combine Sauce Ingredients:
- In a bowl, whisk together BBQ sauce, apple cider vinegar, brown sugar, and Dijon mustard.

Pour Sauce Over Ribs:
- Pour the BBQ sauce mixture over the ribs, making sure to coat them evenly.

Cook on Low:
- Cover and cook on low for 6-7 hours, or until the ribs are tender and easily pull away from the bone.

Optional Step (For Crispy Exterior):
- Preheat your oven broiler. Transfer the cooked ribs to a baking sheet, brush with additional BBQ sauce, and broil for a few minutes until the exterior is crispy.

Serve:

- Serve the BBQ ribs with additional sauce on the side. Enjoy!

These Slow Cooker BBQ Ribs are tender, flavorful, and incredibly easy to make. The slow cooking allows the ribs to absorb the delicious BBQ flavors, resulting in a mouthwatering dish. Enjoy these ribs with your favorite sides for a fantastic meal!

Beef Stroganoff

Ingredients:

- 2 pounds beef stew meat, cut into bite-sized pieces
- Salt and black pepper to taste
- 1 onion, finely chopped
- 3 cloves garlic, minced
- 1 cup beef broth
- 1 tablespoon Worcestershire sauce
- 1 tablespoon Dijon mustard
- 1 teaspoon dried thyme
- 1 teaspoon paprika
- 8 oz mushrooms, sliced
- 1/2 cup sour cream
- 2 tablespoons all-purpose flour
- 1/4 cup water
- Cooked egg noodles or rice, for serving
- Chopped fresh parsley, for garnish (optional)

Instructions:

Season and Brown Beef:
- Season the beef stew meat with salt and black pepper. In a large skillet over medium-high heat, brown the beef on all sides. Transfer the browned beef to the slow cooker.

Add Aromatics and Spices:
- In the same skillet, sauté the chopped onion until translucent. Add minced garlic and sauté for another 30 seconds. Transfer the onion and garlic to the slow cooker. Add beef broth, Worcestershire sauce, Dijon mustard, dried thyme, and paprika. Stir to combine.

Cook on Low:
- Cover and cook on low for 6-8 hours or until the beef is tender.

Add Mushrooms:
- About 30 minutes before serving, add sliced mushrooms to the slow cooker. Stir to combine.

Make Sour Cream Mixture:

- In a small bowl, mix sour cream with flour until well combined. Add 1/4 cup of water and mix until smooth.

Thicken and Finish:
- Stir the sour cream mixture into the slow cooker. Cook for an additional 15-30 minutes until the sauce thickens.

Adjust Seasoning:
- Taste and adjust the seasoning with salt and black pepper if needed.

Serve:
- Serve the beef stroganoff over cooked egg noodles or rice. Garnish with chopped fresh parsley if desired.

This Slow Cooker Beef Stroganoff is creamy, savory, and full of flavor. It's a comforting dish that's perfect for a cozy dinner. Enjoy!

Honey Garlic Chicken

Ingredients:

- 2 pounds boneless, skinless chicken thighs
- Salt and black pepper to taste
- 1/2 cup honey
- 1/4 cup soy sauce
- 3 tablespoons minced garlic
- 1 tablespoon sesame oil
- 1 tablespoon rice vinegar
- 1 teaspoon grated ginger
- 1/4 teaspoon red pepper flakes (optional, for heat)
- 2 tablespoons cornstarch (for later)
- 2 tablespoons water (for later)
- Sesame seeds and chopped green onions for garnish
- Cooked rice, for serving

Instructions:

Season and Brown Chicken:
- Season chicken thighs with salt and black pepper. In a large skillet over medium-high heat, brown the chicken thighs on both sides. Transfer them to the slow cooker.

Prepare Sauce:
- In a bowl, mix together honey, soy sauce, minced garlic, sesame oil, rice vinegar, grated ginger, and red pepper flakes (if using). Pour the sauce over the chicken in the slow cooker.

Cook on Low:
- Cover and cook on low for 3-4 hours or until the chicken is cooked through and tender.

Thicken Sauce:
- In a small bowl, mix cornstarch with water to create a slurry. Stir the slurry into the slow cooker, and continue cooking on low for an additional 30 minutes or until the sauce thickens.

Serve:
- Serve the Honey Garlic Chicken over cooked rice. Garnish with sesame seeds and chopped green onions.

This Slow Cooker Honey Garlic Chicken is sweet, savory, and has a deliciously sticky sauce. It's an easy and hands-off recipe for a tasty weeknight meal. Enjoy!

Italian Meatballs

Ingredients:

For the Meatballs:

- 1 pound ground beef
- 1/2 pound ground pork (or use all beef if preferred)
- 1 cup breadcrumbs
- 1/2 cup grated Parmesan cheese
- 2 cloves garlic, minced
- 1/4 cup fresh parsley, finely chopped
- 2 large eggs
- 1 teaspoon dried oregano
- 1 teaspoon dried basil
- Salt and black pepper to taste

For the Sauce:

- 2 cans (28 oz each) crushed tomatoes
- 1 can (14 oz) diced tomatoes
- 1 onion, finely chopped
- 3 cloves garlic, minced
- 1 teaspoon dried oregano
- 1 teaspoon dried basil
- Salt and black pepper to taste
- 1/4 cup fresh basil, chopped (for garnish)
- Grated Parmesan cheese (for serving)

Instructions:

Make the Meatballs:
- In a large bowl, combine ground beef, ground pork, breadcrumbs, grated Parmesan cheese, minced garlic, chopped parsley, eggs, dried oregano, dried basil, salt, and black pepper. Mix until well combined.

Form Meatballs:
- Shape the mixture into meatballs, about 1 to 1.5 inches in diameter.

Brown Meatballs (Optional):
- If you prefer, you can brown the meatballs in a skillet over medium-high heat for a few minutes on each side until they are lightly browned. This step is optional but can enhance flavor.

Prepare the Sauce:
- In the slow cooker, combine crushed tomatoes, diced tomatoes, chopped onion, minced garlic, dried oregano, dried basil, salt, and black pepper. Stir to combine.

Add Meatballs to Slow Cooker:
- Gently place the meatballs into the sauce in the slow cooker.

Cook on Low:
- Cover and cook on low for 4-6 hours, or until the meatballs are cooked through.

Garnish and Serve:
- Garnish with fresh basil and serve the Italian meatballs over pasta or with crusty bread. Sprinkle with grated Parmesan cheese.

These Slow Cooker Italian Meatballs are flavorful, tender, and perfect for a comforting meal. Enjoy the rich taste of homemade meatballs with minimal effort!

Slow Cooker Pot Roast

Ingredients:

- 3-4 pounds beef chuck roast
- Salt and black pepper to taste
- 2 tablespoons vegetable oil
- 1 onion, chopped
- 3 cloves garlic, minced
- 1 cup beef broth
- 1/2 cup red wine (optional)
- 2 tablespoons tomato paste
- 1 tablespoon Worcestershire sauce
- 1 teaspoon dried thyme
- 1 teaspoon dried rosemary
- 3 large carrots, peeled and cut into chunks
- 3 potatoes, peeled and cut into chunks
- 2 celery stalks, chopped
- 1 cup frozen peas (added later)
- 2 tablespoons cornstarch (optional, for thickening)

Instructions:

Season and Sear the Roast:
- Season the beef chuck roast with salt and black pepper. In a large skillet over medium-high heat, heat vegetable oil. Sear the roast on all sides until browned. Transfer the roast to the slow cooker.

Prepare Sauce:
- In the same skillet, sauté chopped onion and minced garlic until softened. Add beef broth, red wine (if using), tomato paste, Worcestershire sauce, dried thyme, and dried rosemary. Stir to combine.

Cook in Slow Cooker:
- Pour the sauce over the roast in the slow cooker. Add carrots, potatoes, and celery around the roast.

Cook on Low:
- Cover and cook on low for 8 hours or until the roast is fork-tender.

Add Peas:
- About 30 minutes before serving, add frozen peas to the slow cooker.

Optional Thickening:
- If you want a thicker gravy, mix 2 tablespoons of cornstarch with a little water to create a slurry. Stir the slurry into the slow cooker and let it cook for an additional 15-20 minutes until the gravy thickens.

Serve:
- Slice the pot roast and serve it with the vegetables and gravy.

This Slow Cooker Pot Roast is a comforting and satisfying meal. The slow cooking process allows the flavors to meld, resulting in tender meat and flavorful vegetables. Enjoy this classic dish with your favorite sides!

Lemon Herb Chicken

Ingredients:

- 4-6 boneless, skinless chicken breasts
- Salt and black pepper to taste
- 2 tablespoons olive oil
- 4 cloves garlic, minced
- 1 teaspoon dried oregano
- 1 teaspoon dried thyme
- 1 teaspoon dried rosemary
- 1 teaspoon dried basil
- 1/2 teaspoon dried parsley
- Zest and juice of 2 lemons
- 1 cup chicken broth
- 1/4 cup white wine (optional)
- 2 tablespoons chopped fresh parsley (for garnish)
- Lemon slices (for garnish)

Instructions:

Season Chicken:
- Season chicken breasts with salt and black pepper.

Sear Chicken:
- In a large skillet over medium-high heat, heat olive oil. Sear chicken breasts on both sides until browned. Transfer the chicken to the slow cooker.

Prepare Herb Mixture:
- In a small bowl, mix together minced garlic, dried oregano, dried thyme, dried rosemary, dried basil, dried parsley, lemon zest, and lemon juice.

Coat Chicken with Herb Mixture:
- Rub the herb mixture over the seared chicken breasts.

Add Liquid Ingredients:
- Pour chicken broth and white wine (if using) into the slow cooker.

Cook on Low:
- Cover and cook on low for 4-6 hours or until the chicken is cooked through and tender.

Garnish and Serve:

- Garnish the Lemon Herb Chicken with chopped fresh parsley and lemon slices. Serve over rice, pasta, or with your favorite sides.

This Slow Cooker Lemon Herb Chicken is flavorful, tender, and has a delightful citrusy aroma. Enjoy this easy and delicious meal with the bright flavors of lemon and herbs!

Sausage and Peppers

Ingredients:

- 1.5 pounds Italian sausage links (sweet or hot), cut into 2-inch pieces
- 2 bell peppers, thinly sliced (use a mix of colors)
- 1 large onion, thinly sliced
- 3 cloves garlic, minced
- 1 can (14 oz) crushed tomatoes
- 1 can (14 oz) diced tomatoes, drained
- 1 teaspoon dried oregano
- 1 teaspoon dried basil
- 1/2 teaspoon red pepper flakes (optional, for heat)
- Salt and black pepper to taste
- Sub rolls or baguette, for serving
- Grated Parmesan cheese (optional, for serving)
- Chopped fresh parsley (for garnish)

Instructions:

Brown Sausages (Optional):
- If preferred, you can brown the sausage pieces in a skillet over medium-high heat for a few minutes until they are browned on all sides. This step is optional but can enhance flavor.

Combine Ingredients in Slow Cooker:
- In the slow cooker, combine the sliced bell peppers, sliced onion, minced garlic, crushed tomatoes, drained diced tomatoes, dried oregano, dried basil, red pepper flakes (if using), salt, and black pepper. Stir to combine.

Add Sausages:
- Add the sausage pieces to the slow cooker, making sure they are submerged in the sauce.

Cook on Low:
- Cover and cook on low for 4-6 hours, or until the sausages are cooked through and the vegetables are tender.

Serve:
- Serve the sausage and peppers on sub rolls or baguette. Optionally, sprinkle with grated Parmesan cheese and garnish with chopped fresh parsley.

This Slow Cooker Sausage and Peppers is a flavorful and hearty dish that's perfect for sandwiches or served over pasta. Enjoy the combination of savory sausages, sweet bell peppers, and aromatic herbs!

Teriyaki Pork Tenderloin

Ingredients:

- 2 pounds pork tenderloin
- Salt and black pepper to taste
- 1 cup low-sodium soy sauce
- 1/2 cup water
- 1/4 cup brown sugar
- 3 tablespoons honey
- 3 tablespoons rice vinegar
- 3 cloves garlic, minced
- 1 tablespoon grated ginger
- 1 tablespoon sesame oil
- 1 tablespoon cornstarch (optional, for thickening)
- 2 tablespoons water (optional, for thickening)
- Green onions, chopped (for garnish)
- Sesame seeds (for garnish)
- Cooked rice, for serving

Instructions:

Season Pork Tenderloin:
- Season the pork tenderloin with salt and black pepper.

Prepare Teriyaki Sauce:
- In a bowl, whisk together soy sauce, water, brown sugar, honey, rice vinegar, minced garlic, grated ginger, and sesame oil to create the teriyaki sauce.

Place in Slow Cooker:
- Place the seasoned pork tenderloin in the slow cooker. Pour the teriyaki sauce over the pork.

Cook on Low:
- Cover and cook on low for 4-6 hours or until the pork is cooked through and tender.

Optional Thickening:
- If you prefer a thicker sauce, mix cornstarch with water to create a slurry. Stir the slurry into the slow cooker and let it cook for an additional 15-20 minutes until the sauce thickens.

Slice and Serve:
- Slice the teriyaki pork tenderloin and serve it over cooked rice. Spoon some of the sauce over the slices.

Garnish:
- Garnish with chopped green onions and sesame seeds.

This Slow Cooker Teriyaki Pork Tenderloin is a flavorful and tender dish with a sweet and savory sauce. Enjoy it over rice or with your favorite side dishes!

Cuban Mojo Pork

Ingredients:

- 3-4 pounds pork shoulder or pork butt
- Salt and black pepper to taste
- 1 teaspoon cumin
- 1 teaspoon dried oregano
- 1 teaspoon smoked paprika
- 1 onion, thinly sliced
- 4 cloves garlic, minced
- 1 cup orange juice
- 1/2 cup lime juice
- 1/4 cup lemon juice
- Zest of 1 orange
- Zest of 1 lime
- Zest of 1 lemon
- 1/4 cup olive oil
- 1/4 cup chopped fresh cilantro (for garnish)
- Lime wedges (for serving)
- Cooked rice or tortillas (for serving)

Instructions:

Season the Pork:
- Season the pork shoulder or pork butt with salt, black pepper, cumin, dried oregano, and smoked paprika. Rub the seasonings all over the meat.

Place in Slow Cooker:
- Place the seasoned pork in the slow cooker.

Prepare Mojo Sauce:
- In a bowl, combine sliced onion, minced garlic, orange juice, lime juice, lemon juice, orange zest, lime zest, lemon zest, and olive oil. Mix well.

Pour Mojo Sauce Over Pork:
- Pour the mojo sauce over the pork in the slow cooker, making sure to coat the meat evenly.

Cook on Low:
- Cover and cook on low for 6-8 hours or until the pork is fork-tender.

Shred the Pork:

- Once cooked, shred the pork using two forks. Mix it with the flavorful juices in the slow cooker.

Serve:
- Serve the Cuban Mojo Pork over cooked rice or in tortillas. Garnish with chopped cilantro and serve with lime wedges on the side.

This Slow Cooker Cuban Mojo Pork is packed with citrusy and savory flavors. Enjoy the tender and juicy pork with the bright and zesty mojo sauce!

Pork Carnitas

Ingredients:

- 3-4 pounds pork shoulder or pork butt, cut into chunks
- Salt and black pepper to taste
- 1 teaspoon ground cumin
- 1 teaspoon dried oregano
- 1 teaspoon smoked paprika
- 1 teaspoon chili powder
- 1 onion, chopped
- 4 cloves garlic, minced
- 1 jalapeño, seeded and chopped (optional, for heat)
- 1 orange, juiced
- 2 limes, juiced
- 1/4 cup chicken broth
- 2 bay leaves
- Corn tortillas, for serving
- Fresh cilantro, chopped (for garnish)
- Onion, diced (for garnish)
- Lime wedges (for serving)

Instructions:

Season and Sear the Pork:
- Season the pork chunks with salt, black pepper, ground cumin, dried oregano, smoked paprika, and chili powder. In a large skillet over medium-high heat, sear the pork chunks until browned on all sides. Transfer them to the slow cooker.

Add Aromatics:
- In the same skillet, sauté chopped onion, minced garlic, and chopped jalapeño (if using) until softened. Transfer the mixture to the slow cooker.

Juice the Citrus:
- Juice the orange and limes. Pour the citrus juice over the pork in the slow cooker.

Add Liquid Ingredients:
- Add chicken broth and bay leaves to the slow cooker. Stir to combine.

Cook on Low:
- Cover and cook on low for 6-8 hours or until the pork is fork-tender.

Shred the Pork:
- Once cooked, shred the pork using two forks. Remove and discard the bay leaves.

Optional Crisping (Broiler Method):
- Preheat your oven broiler. Transfer the shredded pork to a baking sheet and broil for a few minutes until the edges become crispy.

Serve:
- Serve the Pork Carnitas in corn tortillas. Garnish with chopped fresh cilantro, diced onion, and lime wedges.

These Slow Cooker Pork Carnitas are tender, flavorful, and perfect for making tacos or burritos. Enjoy the rich and savory taste of this classic Mexican dish!

Barbecue Beef Brisket

Ingredients:

- 4-5 pounds beef brisket
- Salt and black pepper to taste
- 1 tablespoon smoked paprika
- 1 tablespoon garlic powder
- 1 tablespoon onion powder
- 1 tablespoon brown sugar
- 1 teaspoon cayenne pepper (adjust to taste)
- 1 cup beef broth
- 1 cup barbecue sauce (plus extra for serving)
- 1/4 cup apple cider vinegar
- 2 tablespoons Worcestershire sauce
- 2 tablespoons Dijon mustard
- 1 tablespoon soy sauce
- 1 onion, sliced
- 4 cloves garlic, minced
- Hamburger buns or rolls, for serving
- Coleslaw, for topping (optional)

Instructions:

Season and Sear Brisket:
- Season the brisket with salt, black pepper, smoked paprika, garlic powder, onion powder, brown sugar, and cayenne pepper. Sear the brisket in a hot skillet until browned on all sides. Transfer it to the slow cooker.

Prepare Barbecue Sauce:
- In a bowl, whisk together beef broth, barbecue sauce, apple cider vinegar, Worcestershire sauce, Dijon mustard, and soy sauce.

Add Aromatics:
- Add sliced onion and minced garlic to the slow cooker.

Pour Barbecue Sauce Over Brisket:
- Pour the barbecue sauce mixture over the brisket in the slow cooker.

Cook on Low:
- Cover and cook on low for 8-10 hours or until the brisket is fork-tender.

Shred Brisket:
- Once cooked, shred the brisket using two forks.

Serve:
- Serve the barbecue beef brisket on hamburger buns or rolls. Top with additional barbecue sauce and coleslaw if desired.

This Slow Cooker Barbecue Beef Brisket is a flavorful and tender dish that's perfect for sandwiches. The slow cooking process allows the brisket to absorb the rich barbecue flavors. Enjoy this classic comfort food with your favorite sides!

Slow Cooker Lamb Curry

Ingredients:

- 2 pounds lamb shoulder, cut into chunks
- Salt and black pepper to taste
- 2 tablespoons vegetable oil
- 2 onions, finely chopped
- 4 cloves garlic, minced
- 1 tablespoon ginger, grated
- 2 tablespoons curry powder
- 1 teaspoon ground cumin
- 1 teaspoon ground coriander
- 1 teaspoon turmeric
- 1/2 teaspoon cayenne pepper (adjust to taste)
- 1 can (14 oz) diced tomatoes
- 1/2 cup tomato paste
- 1 cup coconut milk
- 1 cup beef or vegetable broth
- 2 cinnamon sticks
- 4 cardamom pods
- 4 whole cloves
- 1 bay leaf
- Fresh cilantro, chopped (for garnish)
- Cooked basmati rice, for serving
- Naan bread, for serving

Instructions:

Season and Sear Lamb:
- Season lamb chunks with salt and black pepper. In a large skillet over medium-high heat, heat vegetable oil. Sear the lamb chunks until browned on all sides. Transfer them to the slow cooker.

Sauté Aromatics:
- In the same skillet, sauté chopped onions until softened. Add minced garlic and grated ginger, and cook for an additional minute.

Add Spices:

- Add curry powder, ground cumin, ground coriander, turmeric, and cayenne pepper to the skillet. Stir to coat the onions and aromatics with the spices.

Transfer to Slow Cooker:
- Transfer the onion and spice mixture to the slow cooker with the seared lamb.

Add Tomatoes, Tomato Paste, and Liquid Ingredients:
- Add diced tomatoes, tomato paste, coconut milk, and beef or vegetable broth to the slow cooker.

Add Whole Spices:
- Add cinnamon sticks, cardamom pods, whole cloves, and a bay leaf to the slow cooker.

Cook on Low:
- Cover and cook on low for 6-8 hours or until the lamb is tender and the flavors meld.

Serve:
- Serve the lamb curry over cooked basmati rice, garnished with chopped cilantro. Enjoy with naan bread on the side.

This Slow Cooker Lamb Curry is rich, aromatic, and filled with warm spices. It's a comforting and delicious dish that pairs well with rice or naan bread. Enjoy this flavorful curry!

Beer-Braised Pot Roast

Ingredients:

- 3-4 pounds beef chuck roast
- Salt and black pepper to taste
- 2 tablespoons vegetable oil
- 2 onions, sliced
- 4 cloves garlic, minced
- 2 carrots, sliced
- 2 celery stalks, sliced
- 1 cup beef broth
- 1 cup beer (choose a flavorful beer, like a dark ale or stout)
- 2 tablespoons tomato paste
- 2 tablespoons Worcestershire sauce
- 1 tablespoon Dijon mustard
- 1 teaspoon dried thyme
- 2 bay leaves
- 4-5 medium potatoes, peeled and cut into chunks
- Fresh parsley, chopped (for garnish)

Instructions:

Season and Sear the Roast:
- Season the beef chuck roast with salt and black pepper. In a large skillet over medium-high heat, heat vegetable oil. Sear the roast on all sides until browned. Transfer it to the slow cooker.

Prepare Vegetables:
- In the same skillet, add sliced onions, minced garlic, sliced carrots, and sliced celery. Sauté until the vegetables are slightly softened. Transfer them to the slow cooker.

Combine Broth, Beer, and Flavorings:
- In a bowl, mix beef broth, beer, tomato paste, Worcestershire sauce, Dijon mustard, dried thyme, and bay leaves.

Pour Liquid Mixture Over Roast:
- Pour the liquid mixture over the roast and vegetables in the slow cooker.

Cook on Low:
- Cover and cook on low for 8-10 hours or until the roast is fork-tender.

Add Potatoes:

- About 2 hours before serving, add the peeled and chunked potatoes to the slow cooker.

Serve:
- Once cooked, remove the bay leaves. Slice the pot roast and serve it with the vegetables and potatoes. Garnish with chopped fresh parsley.

This Slow Cooker Beer-Braised Pot Roast is a comforting and savory dish with rich flavors from the beer and aromatic vegetables. Enjoy this hearty meal with your favorite sides!

Asian Pulled Pork Tacos

Ingredients:

- 3-4 pounds pork shoulder or pork butt
- Salt and black pepper to taste
- 1 tablespoon vegetable oil
- 1 onion, sliced
- 4 cloves garlic, minced
- 1/2 cup soy sauce
- 1/4 cup hoisin sauce
- 1/4 cup rice vinegar
- 1/4 cup brown sugar
- 1 tablespoon grated ginger
- 1 teaspoon Chinese five-spice powder
- 1 cup chicken broth
- Flour or corn tortillas, for serving
- Shredded cabbage or slaw mix, for topping
- Sliced green onions, for garnish
- Sesame seeds, for garnish
- Sriracha or your favorite hot sauce, for serving

Instructions:

Season and Sear Pork:
- Season the pork shoulder or pork butt with salt and black pepper. In a large skillet over medium-high heat, heat vegetable oil. Sear the pork on all sides until browned. Transfer it to the slow cooker.

Sauté Aromatics:
- In the same skillet, add sliced onions and minced garlic. Sauté until the onions are softened. Transfer the mixture to the slow cooker.

Prepare Sauce:
- In a bowl, whisk together soy sauce, hoisin sauce, rice vinegar, brown sugar, grated ginger, and Chinese five-spice powder. Pour the sauce over the pork in the slow cooker.

Add Chicken Broth:
- Add chicken broth to the slow cooker, ensuring the pork is partially submerged in the liquid.

Cook on Low:
- Cover and cook on low for 6-8 hours or until the pork is tender and easily shredded.

Shred Pork:
- Once cooked, shred the pork using two forks. Mix the shredded pork with the flavorful juices in the slow cooker.

Assemble Tacos:
- Heat the tortillas. Fill each tortilla with a portion of the pulled pork. Top with shredded cabbage or slaw mix.

Garnish and Serve:
- Garnish the tacos with sliced green onions, sesame seeds, and a drizzle of Sriracha or your favorite hot sauce.

These Slow Cooker Asian Pulled Pork Tacos are a delicious fusion of flavors. Enjoy the tender and savory pulled pork with the crunch of slaw in each bite. Customize with your favorite toppings and savor the goodness!

Vegetarian Delights:
Eggplant Parmesan

Ingredients:

- 2 large eggplants, sliced into 1/2-inch rounds
- Salt
- 2 cups marinara sauce (store-bought or homemade)
- 1 cup breadcrumbs
- 1 cup grated Parmesan cheese
- 2 cups shredded mozzarella cheese
- 2 eggs, beaten
- 1 teaspoon dried oregano
- 1 teaspoon dried basil
- Fresh basil or parsley, chopped (for garnish)

Instructions:

Prepare the Eggplant:
- Sprinkle salt on both sides of the eggplant slices. Allow them to sit for about 30 minutes to draw out excess moisture. Pat the eggplant slices dry with paper towels.

Set Up Breading Station:
- In one bowl, place breadcrumbs. In another bowl, mix grated Parmesan cheese, dried oregano, and dried basil. In a third bowl, beat the eggs.

Bread the Eggplant:
- Dip each eggplant slice into the beaten eggs, then coat with breadcrumbs and the Parmesan mixture.

Layer in the Slow Cooker:
- In the slow cooker, spread a layer of marinara sauce. Place a layer of breaded eggplant slices on top. Repeat the layers, finishing with a layer of marinara sauce on top.

Cook on Low:
- Cover and cook on low for 4-5 hours or until the eggplant is tender.

Add Cheese:
- In the last 30 minutes of cooking, sprinkle shredded mozzarella cheese over the top layer.

Serve:

- Once the cheese is melted and bubbly, carefully scoop out portions of the Eggplant Parmesan. Garnish with fresh basil or parsley.

This Slow Cooker Eggplant Parmesan is a comforting and flavorful dish. Serve it with pasta or a side of crusty bread for a complete meal. Enjoy the layers of eggplant, marinara sauce, and gooey melted cheese!

Vegetarian Bolognese

Ingredients:

- 2 cans (14 oz each) lentils, drained and rinsed (or 2 cups cooked lentils)
- 1 large carrot, finely chopped
- 1 celery stalk, finely chopped
- 1 onion, finely chopped
- 3 cloves garlic, minced
- 1 can (28 oz) crushed tomatoes
- 1 can (14 oz) diced tomatoes
- 1/4 cup tomato paste
- 1/2 cup red wine (optional)
- 2 teaspoons dried oregano
- 2 teaspoons dried basil
- 1 teaspoon dried thyme
- 1 teaspoon dried rosemary
- Salt and black pepper to taste
- 2 bay leaves
- 2 tablespoons olive oil
- 1 cup milk (dairy or plant-based)
- 1/2 cup grated Parmesan cheese (optional)
- 1/4 cup fresh basil or parsley, chopped (for garnish)
- Cooked pasta, for serving

Instructions:

Sauté Vegetables:
- In a skillet, heat olive oil over medium heat. Sauté the chopped carrot, celery, and onion until softened, about 5-7 minutes. Add minced garlic and cook for an additional minute.

Transfer to Slow Cooker:
- Transfer the sautéed vegetables to the slow cooker.

Add Lentils and Tomatoes:
- Add drained lentils, crushed tomatoes, diced tomatoes, and tomato paste to the slow cooker.

Season and Add Wine:
- Stir in dried oregano, dried basil, dried thyme, dried rosemary, salt, and black pepper. If using, pour in the red wine.

Add Bay Leaves:
- Tuck bay leaves into the sauce.

Cook on Low:
- Cover and cook on low for 6-8 hours to allow flavors to meld.

Finish with Milk:
- In the last hour of cooking, stir in the milk. This adds creaminess to the Bolognese.

Adjust Seasoning and Serve:
- Adjust salt and pepper to taste. If desired, stir in Parmesan cheese. Serve the Vegetarian Bolognese over cooked pasta and garnish with chopped fresh basil or parsley.

This Slow Cooker Vegetarian Bolognese is hearty, flavorful, and full of wholesome ingredients. Enjoy it over your favorite pasta for a satisfying and meatless meal!

Crockpot Ratatouille

Ingredients:

- 1 large eggplant, diced
- 2 zucchinis, sliced
- 1 yellow bell pepper, diced
- 1 red bell pepper, diced
- 1 onion, diced
- 3 cloves garlic, minced
- 2 cups diced tomatoes (fresh or canned)
- 1 can (14 oz) tomato sauce
- 1 teaspoon dried thyme
- 1 teaspoon dried oregano
- 1 teaspoon dried basil
- Salt and black pepper to taste
- 2 tablespoons olive oil
- Fresh basil or parsley, chopped (for garnish)

Instructions:

Prepare Vegetables:
- Dice the eggplant, slice the zucchinis, dice the yellow and red bell peppers, dice the onion, and mince the garlic.

Sauté Vegetables:
- In a skillet, heat olive oil over medium heat. Sauté the diced onion and minced garlic until softened. Add the diced eggplant, sliced zucchinis, and diced bell peppers. Cook for an additional 5-7 minutes until the vegetables are slightly tender.

Transfer to Slow Cooker:
- Transfer the sautéed vegetables to the slow cooker.

Add Tomatoes and Sauce:
- Add diced tomatoes, tomato sauce, dried thyme, dried oregano, dried basil, salt, and black pepper to the slow cooker. Stir to combine.

Cook on Low:
- Cover and cook on low for 4-6 hours or until the vegetables are tender.

Adjust Seasoning and Serve:

- Adjust salt and pepper to taste. Serve the Ratatouille hot, garnished with chopped fresh basil or parsley.

Enjoy this Crockpot Ratatouille as a flavorful side dish or as a main course served over rice, quinoa, or pasta. The slow cooking process allows the flavors to meld, creating a delightful and comforting dish.

Slow Cooker Mac and Cheese

Ingredients:

- 2 cups elbow macaroni, uncooked
- 4 cups shredded sharp cheddar cheese
- 1 can (12 oz) evaporated milk
- 1 1/2 cups whole milk
- 1/2 cup unsalted butter, melted
- 1 teaspoon salt
- 1/2 teaspoon black pepper
- 1/2 teaspoon dry mustard
- 1/4 teaspoon garlic powder (optional)
- 1/4 teaspoon onion powder (optional)
- 1/4 cup all-purpose flour

Instructions:

Cook the Macaroni:
- Cook the elbow macaroni according to the package instructions until al dente. Drain and set aside.

Prepare the Cheese Mixture:
- In a large bowl, combine shredded cheddar cheese, evaporated milk, whole milk, melted butter, salt, black pepper, dry mustard, garlic powder (if using), and onion powder (if using). Mix well.

Whisk in Flour:
- Whisk in the all-purpose flour to the cheese mixture until smooth.

Layer in Slow Cooker:
- Grease the slow cooker. Place a layer of cooked macaroni in the slow cooker, followed by a layer of the cheese mixture. Repeat until all the macaroni and cheese mixture are used, ending with a layer of cheese on top.

Cook on Low:
- Cover and cook on low for 2-3 hours, stirring occasionally, until the cheese is melted, and the mac and cheese is creamy.

Adjust Seasoning and Serve:
- Taste and adjust the seasoning if necessary. Serve the slow cooker mac and cheese hot, straight from the slow cooker.

This Slow Cooker Mac and Cheese is creamy, cheesy, and requires minimal effort. It's a perfect side dish for gatherings or a comforting meal on its own. Enjoy!

Quinoa and Vegetable Stew

Ingredients:

- 1 cup quinoa, rinsed
- 4 cups vegetable broth
- 1 can (14 oz) diced tomatoes, undrained
- 2 carrots, sliced
- 2 celery stalks, chopped
- 1 onion, diced
- 2 cloves garlic, minced
- 1 zucchini, diced
- 1 yellow squash, diced
- 1 bell pepper, diced (any color)
- 1 teaspoon dried thyme
- 1 teaspoon dried oregano
- 1 teaspoon ground cumin
- 1/2 teaspoon paprika
- Salt and black pepper to taste
- 2 cups chopped kale or spinach
- 1 can (15 oz) kidney beans, drained and rinsed
- 1 tablespoon olive oil
- Fresh parsley, chopped (for garnish)

Instructions:

Rinse Quinoa:
- Rinse the quinoa under cold water.

Combine Ingredients in Slow Cooker:
- In the slow cooker, combine quinoa, vegetable broth, diced tomatoes, carrots, celery, onion, garlic, zucchini, yellow squash, bell pepper, thyme, oregano, cumin, paprika, salt, and black pepper.

Cook on Low:
- Cover and cook on low for 4-6 hours or until the vegetables are tender and the quinoa is cooked.

Add Kale or Spinach and Beans:
- Stir in the chopped kale or spinach and the drained and rinsed kidney beans during the last 30 minutes of cooking.

Sauté Vegetables:
- In a skillet, heat olive oil over medium heat. Sauté additional vegetables like mushrooms or additional bell peppers until softened. Add them to the slow cooker.

Adjust Seasoning and Serve:
- Taste and adjust the seasoning if needed. Serve the quinoa and vegetable stew hot, garnished with fresh parsley.

This Slow Cooker Quinoa and Vegetable Stew is a hearty and nutritious meal. Packed with a variety of vegetables, quinoa, and beans, it's a wholesome and satisfying dish perfect for a comforting dinner. Enjoy!

Vegetarian Gumbo

Ingredients:

- 1 cup okra, sliced
- 1 large onion, diced
- 1 bell pepper, diced
- 2 celery stalks, diced
- 3 cloves garlic, minced
- 1 can (14 oz) diced tomatoes, undrained
- 1 can (15 oz) kidney beans, drained and rinsed
- 1 cup frozen sliced okra
- 1 cup corn kernels (fresh or frozen)
- 1 cup sliced carrots
- 1 cup sliced okra
- 1 cup chopped collard greens or kale
- 1/2 cup all-purpose flour
- 1/2 cup vegetable oil
- 4 cups vegetable broth
- 2 bay leaves
- 1 teaspoon dried thyme
- 1 teaspoon dried oregano
- 1 teaspoon smoked paprika
- 1 teaspoon cayenne pepper (adjust to taste)
- Salt and black pepper to taste
- Cooked rice, for serving
- Green onions, chopped (for garnish)

Instructions:

Prepare Roux:
- In a skillet over medium heat, combine flour and vegetable oil to make a roux. Stir constantly until the roux becomes a dark brown color, about 15-20 minutes. Be careful not to burn it.

Combine Ingredients in Slow Cooker:
- In the slow cooker, combine diced onions, bell pepper, celery, minced garlic, diced tomatoes, kidney beans, frozen sliced okra, corn, carrots, collard greens or kale, and sliced okra. Stir in the prepared roux.

Add Spices and Broth:

- Pour in vegetable broth and add bay leaves, dried thyme, dried oregano, smoked paprika, cayenne pepper, salt, and black pepper. Stir well to combine.

Cook on Low:
- Cover and cook on low for 6-8 hours, allowing the flavors to meld.

Adjust Seasoning and Serve:
- Taste and adjust the seasoning if needed. Remove the bay leaves before serving.

Serve Over Rice:
- Serve the Vegetarian Gumbo over cooked rice. Garnish with chopped green onions.

This Slow Cooker Vegetarian Gumbo is a flavorful and hearty dish that captures the essence of traditional gumbo without the meat. Enjoy the rich flavors and comforting warmth of this delicious vegetarian version!

Mexican Quinoa Casserole

Ingredients:

- 1 cup quinoa, rinsed
- 1 can (15 oz) black beans, drained and rinsed
- 1 cup corn kernels (fresh or frozen)
- 1 bell pepper, diced (any color)
- 1 onion, diced
- 1 can (14 oz) diced tomatoes, undrained
- 1 can (4 oz) diced green chilies
- 1 cup salsa
- 2 cloves garlic, minced
- 1 teaspoon ground cumin
- 1 teaspoon chili powder
- 1/2 teaspoon paprika
- 1/2 teaspoon dried oregano
- Salt and black pepper to taste
- 2 cups vegetable broth
- 1 cup shredded cheddar or Mexican blend cheese
- Fresh cilantro, chopped (for garnish)
- Avocado slices (for serving)
- Sour cream or Greek yogurt (for serving)

Instructions:

Combine Ingredients in Slow Cooker:
- In the slow cooker, combine quinoa, black beans, corn, diced bell pepper, diced onion, diced tomatoes, diced green chilies, salsa, minced garlic, ground cumin, chili powder, paprika, dried oregano, salt, and black pepper. Stir well to combine.

Add Vegetable Broth:
- Pour in vegetable broth and stir again.

Cook on Low:
- Cover and cook on low for 3-4 hours, or until the quinoa is cooked, and the casserole is heated through.

Add Cheese:
- Sprinkle shredded cheese over the top of the casserole during the last 15-30 minutes of cooking, allowing it to melt.

Serve:
- Once cooked, garnish with chopped fresh cilantro. Serve the Mexican Quinoa Casserole with avocado slices and a dollop of sour cream or Greek yogurt.

This Slow Cooker Mexican Quinoa Casserole is a flavorful and satisfying dish with the goodness of quinoa, beans, vegetables, and Mexican spices. Enjoy the delicious combination of flavors!

Slow Cooker Enchiladas

Ingredients:

- 1 1/2 pounds boneless, skinless chicken breasts
- 1 onion, finely chopped
- 2 cloves garlic, minced
- 1 can (14 oz) black beans, drained and rinsed
- 1 cup corn kernels (fresh or frozen)
- 1 bell pepper, diced
- 1 can (10 oz) red enchilada sauce
- 1 can (4 oz) diced green chilies
- 1 teaspoon ground cumin
- 1 teaspoon chili powder
- 1/2 teaspoon smoked paprika
- Salt and black pepper to taste
- 2 cups shredded Mexican blend cheese
- 8-10 small flour tortillas
- Fresh cilantro, chopped (for garnish)
- Sour cream (for serving)

Instructions:

Prepare Chicken Mixture:
- Place chicken breasts in the slow cooker. Add chopped onion, minced garlic, black beans, corn, diced bell pepper, red enchilada sauce, diced green chilies, ground cumin, chili powder, smoked paprika, salt, and black pepper.

Cook on Low:
- Cover and cook on low for 6-8 hours or until the chicken is cooked through and easily shredded.

Shred Chicken:
- Shred the chicken using two forks and mix it with the other ingredients in the slow cooker.

Assemble Enchiladas:
- Preheat the oven to 375°F (190°C). Grease a baking dish.
- Place a generous spoonful of the chicken mixture in the center of a tortilla, sprinkle with shredded cheese, and roll it up. Place it seam-side down in the prepared baking dish. Repeat with the remaining tortillas.

Bake:
- Once all enchiladas are assembled, pour any remaining sauce from the slow cooker over the top. Sprinkle with additional shredded cheese.
- Bake in the preheated oven for about 20 minutes, or until the cheese is melted and bubbly.

Serve:
- Garnish with chopped cilantro and serve with sour cream on the side.

These Slow Cooker Chicken Enchiladas are a convenient way to enjoy the flavors of enchiladas without much fuss. Customize with your favorite toppings and enjoy a delicious and hearty meal!

Vegetarian Tikka Masala

Ingredients:

For the Tikka Masala Sauce:

- 1 large onion, finely chopped
- 3 cloves garlic, minced
- 1 tablespoon fresh ginger, grated
- 1 can (14 oz) diced tomatoes
- 1 can (14 oz) tomato sauce
- 1 cup plain yogurt (Greek or plant-based)
- 2 teaspoons garam masala
- 1 teaspoon ground coriander
- 1 teaspoon ground cumin
- 1 teaspoon turmeric
- 1 teaspoon smoked paprika
- 1/2 teaspoon cayenne pepper (adjust to taste)
- Salt and black pepper to taste
- 1/2 cup heavy cream or coconut cream

For the Vegetables:

- 2 cups mixed vegetables (e.g., cauliflower, bell peppers, peas, carrots), chopped
- 1 can (15 oz) chickpeas, drained and rinsed

Instructions:

Prepare Tikka Masala Sauce:
- In a blender, combine chopped onion, minced garlic, grated ginger, diced tomatoes, tomato sauce, yogurt, garam masala, ground coriander, ground cumin, turmeric, smoked paprika, cayenne pepper, salt, and black pepper. Blend until smooth.

Combine Sauce and Vegetables in Slow Cooker:
- Place mixed vegetables and chickpeas in the slow cooker. Pour the blended Tikka Masala sauce over the vegetables and chickpeas. Stir to combine.

Cook on Low:
- Cover and cook on low for 4-6 hours or until the vegetables are tender.

Finish with Cream:
- About 30 minutes before serving, stir in the heavy cream or coconut cream. This adds richness to the dish.

Adjust Seasoning and Serve:
- Taste and adjust the seasoning if needed. Serve the Vegetarian Tikka Masala over rice or with naan bread. Garnish with fresh cilantro.

This Slow Cooker Vegetarian Tikka Masala is a flavorful and comforting dish that brings together a rich and creamy sauce with a variety of vegetables. Enjoy the aromatic and spicy flavors of this classic Indian dish!

Vegetable Lasagna

Ingredients:

- 1 box (about 9 oz) no-boil lasagna noodles
- 2 cups ricotta cheese
- 1 egg
- 1 cup grated Parmesan cheese
- 3 cups shredded mozzarella cheese
- 1 zucchini, thinly sliced
- 1 yellow squash, thinly sliced
- 1 bell pepper, thinly sliced
- 1 carrot, peeled and thinly sliced
- 1 onion, finely chopped
- 3 cloves garlic, minced
- 1 can (28 oz) crushed tomatoes
- 1 can (14 oz) tomato sauce
- 1 can (6 oz) tomato paste
- 1 teaspoon dried oregano
- 1 teaspoon dried basil
- 1/2 teaspoon dried thyme
- Salt and black pepper to taste
- Fresh basil or parsley, chopped (for garnish)

Instructions:

Prepare Vegetable Filling:
- In a skillet, sauté chopped onion and minced garlic until softened. Add sliced zucchini, yellow squash, bell pepper, and carrot. Cook for an additional 5-7 minutes until vegetables are slightly tender. Set aside.

Prepare Cheese Mixture:
- In a bowl, combine ricotta cheese, egg, and grated Parmesan cheese. Mix well.

Prepare Tomato Sauce:
- In another bowl, mix crushed tomatoes, tomato sauce, tomato paste, dried oregano, dried basil, dried thyme, salt, and black pepper.

Assemble Lasagna:
- Grease the slow cooker. Spread a layer of tomato sauce at the bottom.
- Place a layer of no-boil lasagna noodles over the sauce.

- Add a layer of the ricotta mixture, followed by a layer of the sautéed vegetables. Sprinkle mozzarella cheese over the vegetables.
- Repeat the layers until all ingredients are used, finishing with a layer of tomato sauce and a generous sprinkle of mozzarella cheese on top.

Cook on Low:
- Cover and cook on low for 3-4 hours or until the noodles are tender and the cheese is melted.

Let it Rest:
- Turn off the slow cooker and let the vegetable lasagna rest for about 15-20 minutes before serving.

Garnish and Serve:
- Garnish with chopped fresh basil or parsley before serving.

This Slow Cooker Vegetable Lasagna is a convenient way to enjoy a classic Italian dish with layers of pasta, rich tomato sauce, cheesy goodness, and a variety of vegetables. Enjoy the comfort of lasagna without turning on the oven!

Vegan Butternut Squash Curry

Ingredients:

- 1 medium butternut squash, peeled, seeded, and diced
- 1 can (15 oz) chickpeas, drained and rinsed
- 1 onion, finely chopped
- 3 cloves garlic, minced
- 1 can (14 oz) diced tomatoes
- 1 can (14 oz) coconut milk
- 1 cup vegetable broth
- 2 tablespoons red curry paste
- 1 tablespoon curry powder
- 1 teaspoon ground turmeric
- 1 teaspoon ground cumin
- 1 teaspoon ground coriander
- 1 teaspoon ginger, grated
- Salt and black pepper to taste
- 2 cups baby spinach or kale
- Fresh cilantro, chopped (for garnish)
- Cooked rice or naan bread (for serving)

Instructions:

Combine Ingredients in Slow Cooker:
- In the slow cooker, combine diced butternut squash, chickpeas, chopped onion, minced garlic, diced tomatoes, coconut milk, vegetable broth, red curry paste, curry powder, turmeric, cumin, coriander, grated ginger, salt, and black pepper. Stir well to combine.

Cook on Low:
- Cover and cook on low for 4-6 hours, or until the butternut squash is tender.

Add Greens:
- About 30 minutes before serving, stir in baby spinach or kale. This adds freshness and nutritional value to the curry.

Adjust Seasoning and Serve:
- Taste and adjust the seasoning if needed. Serve the Vegan Butternut Squash Curry over cooked rice or with naan bread. Garnish with chopped fresh cilantro.

This Slow Cooker Vegan Butternut Squash Curry is a flavorful and comforting dish with the sweetness of butternut squash, the creaminess of coconut milk, and the warmth of curry spices. Enjoy a delicious and nutritious plant-based meal!

Slow Cooker Eggplant Lasagna

Ingredients:

- 2 large eggplants, thinly sliced lengthwise
- Salt, for salting eggplant slices
- 1 pound ground beef or plant-based ground meat alternative
- 1 onion, finely chopped
- 3 cloves garlic, minced
- 1 can (14 oz) crushed tomatoes
- 1 can (14 oz) tomato sauce
- 1 can (6 oz) tomato paste
- 2 teaspoons dried oregano
- 2 teaspoons dried basil
- 1 teaspoon dried thyme
- Salt and black pepper to taste
- 2 cups ricotta cheese
- 1/2 cup grated Parmesan cheese
- 2 cups shredded mozzarella cheese
- Fresh basil or parsley, chopped (for garnish)
- Cooking spray

Instructions:

Prepare Eggplant:
- Thinly slice the eggplant lengthwise. Lay the slices on a baking sheet and sprinkle with salt. Allow them to sit for about 30 minutes to draw out excess moisture. Pat them dry with paper towels.

Brown Ground Beef:
- In a skillet over medium heat, brown the ground beef or plant-based ground meat alternative. Drain excess fat.

Prepare Tomato Sauce:
- In a bowl, combine crushed tomatoes, tomato sauce, tomato paste, dried oregano, dried basil, dried thyme, salt, and black pepper. Mix well.

Layer in Slow Cooker:
- Spray the slow cooker with cooking spray. Start by layering eggplant slices at the bottom.
- Add a layer of the tomato sauce mixture, followed by a layer of browned ground beef or plant-based alternative.

- Dollop ricotta cheese over the meat layer and sprinkle with Parmesan and mozzarella cheese.
- Repeat the layers until all ingredients are used, finishing with a layer of cheese on top.

Cook on Low:
- Cover and cook on low for 4-6 hours or until the eggplant is tender and the cheese is melted.

Let it Rest:
- Turn off the slow cooker and let the eggplant lasagna rest for about 15-20 minutes before serving.

Garnish and Serve:
- Garnish with chopped fresh basil or parsley. Serve the Slow Cooker Eggplant Lasagna warm.

This Slow Cooker Eggplant Lasagna is a delicious and low-carb twist on traditional lasagna. Enjoy the layers of flavorful tomato sauce, cheesy goodness, and tender eggplant slices!

Chickpea and Vegetable Curry

Ingredients:

- 2 cans (15 oz each) chickpeas, drained and rinsed
- 1 large sweet potato, peeled and diced
- 1 cauliflower, cut into florets
- 1 red bell pepper, diced
- 1 yellow bell pepper, diced
- 1 onion, finely chopped
- 3 cloves garlic, minced
- 1 can (14 oz) diced tomatoes
- 1 can (14 oz) coconut milk
- 1 cup vegetable broth
- 2 tablespoons curry powder
- 1 tablespoon ground cumin
- 1 tablespoon ground coriander
- 1 teaspoon turmeric
- 1 teaspoon paprika
- 1 teaspoon ginger, grated
- Salt and black pepper to taste
- 2 cups spinach or kale
- Fresh cilantro, chopped (for garnish)
- Cooked rice or naan bread (for serving)

Instructions:

Combine Ingredients in Slow Cooker:
- In the slow cooker, combine chickpeas, diced sweet potato, cauliflower florets, diced red bell pepper, diced yellow bell pepper, chopped onion, minced garlic, diced tomatoes, coconut milk, vegetable broth, curry powder, cumin, coriander, turmeric, paprika, grated ginger, salt, and black pepper. Stir well to combine.

Cook on Low:
- Cover and cook on low for 4-6 hours, or until the vegetables are tender.

Add Greens:
- About 30 minutes before serving, stir in spinach or kale. This adds freshness and nutritional value to the curry.

Adjust Seasoning and Serve:
- Taste and adjust the seasoning if needed. Serve the Chickpea and Vegetable Curry over cooked rice or with naan bread. Garnish with chopped fresh cilantro.

This Slow Cooker Chickpea and Vegetable Curry is a wholesome and flavorful dish packed with a variety of vegetables and the protein-rich goodness of chickpeas. Enjoy the aromatic and comforting flavors of this plant-based curry!

Slow Cooker Sweet Potato and Quinoa Stew

Ingredients:

- 2 large sweet potatoes, peeled and diced
- 1 cup quinoa, rinsed
- 1 can (15 oz) black beans, drained and rinsed
- 1 can (14 oz) diced tomatoes
- 1 onion, finely chopped
- 3 cloves garlic, minced
- 1 bell pepper, diced
- 4 cups vegetable broth
- 1 teaspoon ground cumin
- 1 teaspoon smoked paprika
- 1/2 teaspoon ground coriander
- 1/2 teaspoon chili powder
- Salt and black pepper to taste
- 2 cups kale or spinach, chopped
- 1 cup corn kernels (fresh or frozen)
- Fresh cilantro, chopped (for garnish)
- Avocado slices (for serving)

Instructions:

Combine Ingredients in Slow Cooker:
- In the slow cooker, combine diced sweet potatoes, rinsed quinoa, black beans, diced tomatoes, chopped onion, minced garlic, diced bell pepper, vegetable broth, ground cumin, smoked paprika, ground coriander, chili powder, salt, and black pepper. Stir well to combine.

Cook on Low:
- Cover and cook on low for 4-6 hours, or until the sweet potatoes are tender.

Add Greens and Corn:
- About 30 minutes before serving, stir in chopped kale or spinach and corn kernels. This adds freshness and nutritional value to the stew.

Adjust Seasoning and Serve:
- Taste and adjust the seasoning if needed. Serve the Sweet Potato and Quinoa Stew hot, garnished with chopped fresh cilantro and topped with avocado slices.

This Slow Cooker Sweet Potato and Quinoa Stew is a hearty and nutritious dish that combines the natural sweetness of sweet potatoes with the protein-packed quinoa and an array of flavorful spices. Enjoy this wholesome and comforting stew!

Vegan Lentil Sloppy Joes

Ingredients:

- 1 cup dry green or brown lentils, rinsed and drained
- 1 onion, finely chopped
- 2 bell peppers, diced
- 3 cloves garlic, minced
- 1 can (14 oz) crushed tomatoes
- 1/4 cup tomato paste
- 1/4 cup soy sauce or tamari
- 2 tablespoons maple syrup or agave nectar
- 1 tablespoon Dijon mustard
- 1 tablespoon chili powder
- 1 teaspoon ground cumin
- 1 teaspoon smoked paprika
- 1/2 teaspoon dried oregano
- Salt and black pepper to taste
- Hamburger buns or your preferred bread
- Coleslaw or pickles (optional, for serving)

Instructions:

Combine Ingredients in Slow Cooker:
- In the slow cooker, combine rinsed lentils, chopped onion, diced bell peppers, minced garlic, crushed tomatoes, tomato paste, soy sauce or tamari, maple syrup or agave nectar, Dijon mustard, chili powder, ground cumin, smoked paprika, dried oregano, salt, and black pepper. Stir well to combine.

Cook on Low:
- Cover and cook on low for 6-8 hours, or until the lentils are tender.

Adjust Seasoning:
- Taste and adjust the seasoning if needed.

Serve:
- Spoon the lentil mixture onto hamburger buns or your preferred bread. Serve with coleslaw or pickles if desired.

These Slow Cooker Vegan Lentil Sloppy Joes are a delicious and plant-based twist on the classic comfort food. Packed with protein-rich lentils and flavorful seasonings, they make for a satisfying and wholesome meal. Enjoy!

Slow Cooker Ratatouille

Ingredients:

- 1 large eggplant, diced
- 2 zucchini, sliced
- 1 yellow bell pepper, sliced
- 1 red bell pepper, sliced
- 1 onion, thinly sliced
- 3 cloves garlic, minced
- 1 can (14 oz) diced tomatoes
- 1 can (6 oz) tomato paste
- 2 tablespoons olive oil
- 1 teaspoon dried thyme
- 1 teaspoon dried rosemary
- 1 teaspoon dried oregano
- Salt and black pepper to taste
- Fresh basil or parsley, chopped (for garnish)

Instructions:

Combine Ingredients in Slow Cooker:
- In the slow cooker, combine diced eggplant, sliced zucchini, sliced yellow bell pepper, sliced red bell pepper, thinly sliced onion, minced garlic, diced tomatoes, tomato paste, olive oil, dried thyme, dried rosemary, dried oregano, salt, and black pepper. Stir well to combine.

Cook on Low:
- Cover and cook on low for 6-8 hours, or until the vegetables are tender.

Adjust Seasoning:
- Taste and adjust the seasoning if needed.

Serve:
- Spoon the ratatouille onto plates and garnish with chopped fresh basil or parsley.

This Slow Cooker Ratatouille is a classic French dish with a medley of colorful vegetables and aromatic herbs. Enjoy it as a side dish or as a main course served over rice or pasta.

Vegan Black Bean and Pumpkin Chili

Ingredients:

- 2 cans (15 oz each) black beans, drained and rinsed
- 1 can (15 oz) pumpkin puree
- 1 can (14 oz) diced tomatoes
- 1 onion, chopped
- 3 cloves garlic, minced
- 1 bell pepper, diced
- 1 jalapeño, finely chopped (optional, for heat)
- 1 cup corn kernels (fresh or frozen)
- 4 cups vegetable broth
- 2 tablespoons chili powder
- 1 tablespoon cumin
- 1 teaspoon smoked paprika
- 1 teaspoon oregano
- Salt and black pepper to taste
- Juice of 1 lime
- Fresh cilantro, chopped (for garnish)
- Avocado slices (for serving)
- Vegan sour cream (optional, for serving)

Instructions:

Combine Ingredients in Slow Cooker:
- In the slow cooker, combine black beans, pumpkin puree, diced tomatoes, chopped onion, minced garlic, diced bell pepper, chopped jalapeño (if using), corn kernels, vegetable broth, chili powder, cumin, smoked paprika, oregano, salt, and black pepper. Stir well to combine.

Cook on Low:
- Cover and cook on low for 6-8 hours, allowing the flavors to meld.

Adjust Seasoning:
- Taste and adjust the seasoning if needed. Add lime juice and stir.

Serve:
- Ladle the chili into bowls and garnish with chopped fresh cilantro. Top with avocado slices and vegan sour cream if desired.

This Slow Cooker Vegan Black Bean and Pumpkin Chili is a comforting and flavorful dish with the richness of black beans and the autumnal touch of pumpkin. Enjoy a warm and hearty bowl on a chilly day!

Slow Cooker Cauliflower Curry

Ingredients:

- 1 large cauliflower, cut into florets
- 1 can (14 oz) chickpeas, drained and rinsed
- 1 onion, finely chopped
- 3 cloves garlic, minced
- 1 can (14 oz) diced tomatoes
- 1 can (14 oz) coconut milk
- 1 cup vegetable broth
- 2 tablespoons curry powder
- 1 tablespoon ground cumin
- 1 tablespoon ground coriander
- 1 teaspoon turmeric
- 1 teaspoon ginger, grated
- 1/2 teaspoon cayenne pepper (adjust to taste)
- Salt and black pepper to taste
- 2 cups spinach or kale, chopped
- Fresh cilantro, chopped (for garnish)
- Cooked rice or naan bread (for serving)

Instructions:

Combine Ingredients in Slow Cooker:
- In the slow cooker, combine cauliflower florets, chickpeas, chopped onion, minced garlic, diced tomatoes, coconut milk, vegetable broth, curry powder, cumin, coriander, turmeric, grated ginger, cayenne pepper, salt, and black pepper. Stir well to combine.

Cook on Low:
- Cover and cook on low for 4-6 hours, or until the cauliflower is tender.

Add Greens:
- About 30 minutes before serving, stir in chopped spinach or kale. This adds freshness and nutritional value to the curry.

Adjust Seasoning and Serve:
- Taste and adjust the seasoning if needed. Serve the Slow Cooker Cauliflower Curry over cooked rice or with naan bread. Garnish with chopped fresh cilantro.

This Slow Cooker Cauliflower Curry is a delicious and convenient way to enjoy the flavors of a classic curry with the added goodness of cauliflower. Enjoy this flavorful and comforting dish!

Vegetarian Cabbage Rolls

Ingredients:

For the Filling:

- 1 cup cooked brown rice
- 1 can (15 oz) black beans, drained and rinsed
- 1 cup corn kernels (fresh or frozen)
- 1 onion, finely chopped
- 2 cloves garlic, minced
- 1 teaspoon ground cumin
- 1 teaspoon smoked paprika
- Salt and black pepper to taste
- 1 cup tomato sauce

For the Cabbage Rolls:

- 1 large head of cabbage
- Tomato sauce for layering

For the Sauce:

- 2 cans (14 oz each) diced tomatoes
- 1 can (6 oz) tomato paste
- 1 teaspoon dried oregano
- 1 teaspoon dried basil
- Salt and black pepper to taste

Instructions:

Prepare the Cabbage Leaves:
- Bring a large pot of water to a boil. Carefully immerse the whole head of cabbage into the boiling water. After a few minutes, carefully peel off the outer leaves. Repeat until you have about 12-15 large leaves.

Prepare the Filling:
- In a bowl, combine cooked brown rice, black beans, corn, chopped onion, minced garlic, ground cumin, smoked paprika, salt, and black pepper. Mix well. Stir in 1 cup of tomato sauce.

Prepare the Sauce:

- In another bowl, mix diced tomatoes, tomato paste, dried oregano, dried basil, salt, and black pepper.

Assemble the Cabbage Rolls:
- Place a cabbage leaf on a flat surface. Spoon a portion of the filling onto the center of the leaf. Fold in the sides and roll up the cabbage leaf. Repeat with the remaining leaves and filling.

Layer in Slow Cooker:
- Spread a thin layer of the sauce in the bottom of the slow cooker. Place the cabbage rolls on top, seam side down. Continue layering until all cabbage rolls are in the slow cooker.

Pour Sauce Over the Top:
- Pour the remaining sauce over the top of the cabbage rolls.

Cook on Low:
- Cover and cook on low for 6-8 hours, or until the cabbage is tender.

Serve:
- Carefully remove the cabbage rolls from the slow cooker and place them on a serving platter. Spoon some of the tomato sauce over the top. Serve warm.

These Slow Cooker Vegetarian Cabbage Rolls are a tasty and satisfying meatless version of a classic dish. Enjoy the combination of flavorful filling and tender cabbage cooked to perfection!

Vegan Moroccan Chickpea Tagine

Ingredients:

- 2 cans (15 oz each) chickpeas, drained and rinsed
- 1 large sweet potato, peeled and diced
- 1 onion, finely chopped
- 3 cloves garlic, minced
- 1 can (14 oz) diced tomatoes
- 1 cup vegetable broth
- 1 cup dried apricots, chopped
- 1/2 cup green olives, sliced
- 1/4 cup tomato paste
- 2 tablespoons olive oil
- 1 tablespoon ground cumin
- 1 tablespoon ground coriander
- 1 tablespoon smoked paprika
- 1 teaspoon ground cinnamon
- 1 teaspoon ground turmeric
- 1/2 teaspoon cayenne pepper (adjust to taste)
- Salt and black pepper to taste
- Fresh cilantro, chopped (for garnish)
- Cooked couscous or rice (for serving)

Instructions:

Combine Ingredients in Slow Cooker:
- In the slow cooker, combine chickpeas, diced sweet potato, chopped onion, minced garlic, diced tomatoes, vegetable broth, chopped dried apricots, sliced green olives, tomato paste, olive oil, ground cumin, ground coriander, smoked paprika, ground cinnamon, ground turmeric, cayenne pepper, salt, and black pepper. Stir well to combine.

Cook on Low:
- Cover and cook on low for 6-8 hours, or until the sweet potatoes are tender.

Adjust Seasoning:
- Taste and adjust the seasoning if needed.

Serve:

- Spoon the Moroccan Chickpea Tagine over cooked couscous or rice. Garnish with chopped fresh cilantro.

This Slow Cooker Vegan Moroccan Chickpea Tagine is a flavorful and aromatic dish with a perfect blend of spices and textures. Enjoy the exotic flavors of Morocco in this easy and hearty slow cooker recipe!

Soups and Stews:
Slow Cooker Apple Crisp

Ingredients:

For the Apple Filling:

- 6 cups apples, peeled, cored, and sliced (a mix of sweet and tart apples)
- 1/2 cup granulated sugar
- 1 teaspoon ground cinnamon
- 1/4 teaspoon ground nutmeg
- 1 tablespoon lemon juice

For the Crumb Topping:

- 1 cup old-fashioned oats
- 1/2 cup all-purpose flour
- 1/2 cup brown sugar, packed
- 1/2 cup unsalted butter, softened
- 1/2 teaspoon ground cinnamon
- 1/4 teaspoon salt

Optional for serving:

- Vanilla ice cream or whipped cream

Instructions:

Prepare the Apple Filling:
- In a large bowl, combine sliced apples, granulated sugar, ground cinnamon, ground nutmeg, and lemon juice. Toss until the apples are evenly coated.

Assemble in Slow Cooker:
- Place the apple mixture in the slow cooker, spreading it out evenly.

Prepare the Crumb Topping:
- In a separate bowl, combine oats, all-purpose flour, brown sugar, softened butter, ground cinnamon, and salt. Mix until the mixture resembles coarse crumbs.

Add Crumb Topping:

- Sprinkle the crumb topping evenly over the apples in the slow cooker.

Cook:
- Cover the slow cooker and cook on low for 3-4 hours, or until the apples are tender.

Serve:
- Scoop the apple crisp into serving bowls. Optionally, serve with a scoop of vanilla ice cream or a dollop of whipped cream.

Enjoy this warm and comforting Slow Cooker Apple Crisp with its tender, cinnamon-spiced apples and crunchy oat topping!

Chocolate Lava Cake

Ingredients:

- 1 cup all-purpose flour
- 1/2 cup cocoa powder
- 1 1/2 cups granulated sugar
- 1/2 teaspoon baking powder
- 1/4 teaspoon salt
- 1/2 cup unsalted butter, melted
- 1/2 cup milk
- 1 teaspoon vanilla extract

For the Lava Center:

- 1/2 cup semisweet chocolate chips
- 1/4 cup granulated sugar
- 1/4 cup hot water

Instructions:

Prepare Slow Cooker:
- Grease the inside of your slow cooker with butter or non-stick cooking spray.

Make the Batter:
- In a bowl, whisk together the flour, cocoa powder, sugar, baking powder, and salt.
- Add melted butter, milk, and vanilla extract to the dry ingredients. Stir until just combined. The batter will be thick.

Prepare Lava Center:
- In a separate bowl, mix together the chocolate chips, sugar, and hot water until the chocolate chips are melted.

Assemble in Slow Cooker:
- Pour the chocolate batter into the prepared slow cooker.
- Spoon the chocolate lava mixture evenly over the batter. Do not stir.

Cook:
- Cover the slow cooker with a lid and cook on low for 2-3 hours, or until the edges are set but the center is still slightly gooey.

Serve:

- Scoop out portions of the Chocolate Lava Cake and serve warm. You can add a scoop of vanilla ice cream or a dusting of powdered sugar on top if desired.

Enjoy the rich and gooey goodness of this Slow Cooker Chocolate Lava Cake!

Slow Cooker Rice Pudding

Ingredients:

- 1 cup white rice (short-grain or long-grain)
- 2 cups milk (whole milk or a combination of milk and heavy cream for a richer pudding)
- 1/2 cup granulated sugar
- 1/2 teaspoon vanilla extract
- 1/4 teaspoon ground cinnamon
- 1/4 teaspoon ground nutmeg
- Pinch of salt
- 1/2 cup raisins (optional)

Instructions:

Rinse Rice:
- Rinse the rice under cold water until the water runs clear.

Combine Ingredients in Slow Cooker:
- In the slow cooker, combine the rinsed rice, milk, granulated sugar, vanilla extract, ground cinnamon, ground nutmeg, and a pinch of salt. Stir to combine.

Add Raisins (Optional):
- If using raisins, add them to the mixture and stir.

Cook:
- Cover the slow cooker with a lid and cook on low for 2-3 hours or until the rice is tender and the pudding has thickened. Stir occasionally to prevent sticking.

Serve:
- Once the rice pudding reaches the desired consistency, turn off the slow cooker. If you prefer a thicker pudding, you can let it sit with the lid off for a bit.

Enjoy:
- Serve the rice pudding warm or chilled. Optionally, sprinkle a bit of cinnamon on top before serving.

Feel free to adjust the sweetness and spice levels to your liking. This Slow Cooker Rice Pudding is a comforting and easy dessert that can be enjoyed on its own or with your favorite toppings.

Peach Cobbler

Ingredients:

For the Peach Filling:

- 6 cups fresh or canned peaches, sliced
- 1/2 cup granulated sugar
- 1/4 cup brown sugar
- 1 teaspoon ground cinnamon
- 1/4 teaspoon ground nutmeg
- 1 tablespoon cornstarch (if using fresh peaches)

For the Cobbler Topping:

- 1 cup all-purpose flour
- 1/2 cup granulated sugar
- 1/2 cup brown sugar
- 1 teaspoon baking powder
- 1/2 teaspoon salt
- 1/2 cup unsalted butter, melted
- 1/3 cup boiling water

Instructions:

Prepare the Slow Cooker:
- Grease the inside of your slow cooker with butter or non-stick cooking spray.

Prepare the Peach Filling:
- In a large bowl, combine sliced peaches, granulated sugar, brown sugar, ground cinnamon, and ground nutmeg. If using fresh peaches, toss them with cornstarch to help thicken the filling.

Assemble in Slow Cooker:
- Pour the peach mixture into the prepared slow cooker, spreading it out evenly.

Prepare the Cobbler Topping:

- In another bowl, whisk together flour, granulated sugar, brown sugar, baking powder, and salt.
- Add melted butter and stir until combined. The mixture will be crumbly.
- Spread the crumbly mixture over the peaches in the slow cooker.

Add Boiling Water:
- Pour boiling water evenly over the cobbler topping. Do not stir.

Cook:
- Cover the slow cooker with a lid and cook on high for 2-3 hours or until the cobbler topping is set.

Serve:
- Scoop out portions of the peach cobbler and serve warm. You can enjoy it as is or with a scoop of vanilla ice cream.

This Slow Cooker Peach Cobbler is a delightful dessert that captures the sweetness of ripe peaches and the comforting taste of a classic cobbler. Enjoy!

Caramelized Bananas

Ingredients:

- 2 ripe bananas, peeled and sliced
- 2 tablespoons unsalted butter
- 2 tablespoons brown sugar
- 1 teaspoon vanilla extract
- Pinch of salt
- Optional toppings: vanilla ice cream, chopped nuts, or a sprinkle of cinnamon

Instructions:

Slice the Bananas:
- Peel the bananas and slice them into rounds.

Caramelize the Bananas:
- In a skillet or pan, melt the butter over medium heat.
- Add the brown sugar to the melted butter and stir until the sugar has dissolved.
- Add the sliced bananas to the skillet, arranging them in a single layer.
- Cook the bananas for 2-3 minutes on each side, or until they become golden and caramelized.

Add Flavorings:
- Drizzle vanilla extract over the caramelized bananas and sprinkle a pinch of salt. Toss gently to coat the bananas evenly.

Serve:
- Transfer the caramelized bananas to a serving plate.
- Optionally, serve the caramelized bananas over vanilla ice cream, topped with chopped nuts or a sprinkle of cinnamon.

Caramelized bananas are a quick and delicious treat that can be enjoyed on their own or used as a topping for various desserts. Enjoy the sweet and gooey goodness!

Slow Cooker Bread Pudding

Ingredients:

For the Bread Pudding:

- 6 cups stale bread, cubed (challah, brioche, or French bread work well)
- 2 cups milk
- 4 large eggs
- 1 cup granulated sugar
- 1/4 cup unsalted butter, melted
- 1 teaspoon vanilla extract
- 1/2 teaspoon ground cinnamon
- 1/4 teaspoon ground nutmeg
- 1/2 cup raisins or chocolate chips (optional)

For the Sauce:

- 1/2 cup unsalted butter
- 1 cup packed brown sugar
- 2 tablespoons heavy cream
- 1 teaspoon vanilla extract
- Pinch of salt

Instructions:

Prepare the Slow Cooker:
- Grease the inside of your slow cooker with butter or non-stick cooking spray.

Make the Bread Pudding:
- In a large bowl, whisk together the eggs, milk, granulated sugar, melted butter, vanilla extract, ground cinnamon, and ground nutmeg.
- Add the cubed bread to the egg mixture, ensuring that all the bread is coated. Let it sit for about 15 minutes to allow the bread to absorb the liquid. Add raisins or chocolate chips if using.

Assemble in Slow Cooker:
- Transfer the soaked bread mixture to the prepared slow cooker, spreading it out evenly.

Cook the Bread Pudding:

- Cover the slow cooker with a lid and cook on low for 3-4 hours, or until the center is set and the edges are golden.

Make the Sauce:
- In a saucepan, melt the butter for the sauce. Add brown sugar, heavy cream, vanilla extract, and a pinch of salt. Stir until the sugar is dissolved, and the sauce is smooth.

Serve:
- Drizzle the warm sauce over the individual servings of bread pudding.

This Slow Cooker Bread Pudding is a comforting and delicious dessert, perfect for cozy evenings. Enjoy the rich, custardy texture and the sweet, buttery sauce!

Chocolate Fondue

Ingredients:

- 8 ounces (about 225 grams) good-quality dark chocolate, finely chopped
- 1 cup heavy cream
- 1 teaspoon pure vanilla extract
- Dipping items (strawberries, banana slices, marshmallows, pretzels, etc.)

Instructions:

Prepare Dipping Items:
- Wash and cut fruits into bite-sized pieces. Arrange an assortment of dipping items on a serving platter.

Chop Chocolate:
- Finely chop the dark chocolate. The finer it's chopped, the quicker it will melt.

Heat the Cream:
- In a saucepan over medium heat, warm the heavy cream until it begins to simmer. Be careful not to let it boil.

Melt Chocolate:
- Place the chopped chocolate in a heatproof bowl. Pour the hot cream over the chocolate. Let it sit for a minute to soften the chocolate.
- Stir the mixture until the chocolate is completely melted and smooth. If needed, you can gently heat the mixture over low heat while stirring.

Add Vanilla:
- Stir in the vanilla extract.

Transfer to Fondue Pot or Serving Dish:
- Transfer the melted chocolate to a fondue pot or a heatproof serving dish.

Serve:
- Arrange the dipping items around the chocolate fondue pot. Provide fondue forks or skewers for dipping.

Enjoy:
- Dip your chosen items into the melted chocolate and savor the deliciousness!

Feel free to get creative with the dipping items, and enjoy this chocolate fondue for a fun and indulgent dessert experience.

Berry Compote

Ingredients:

- 2 cups mixed berries (strawberries, blueberries, raspberries, blackberries)
- 1/4 cup granulated sugar (adjust based on sweetness preference and the sweetness of the berries)
- 1 tablespoon fresh lemon juice
- 1 teaspoon cornstarch (optional, for thickening)

Instructions:

Prepare the Berries:
- If using strawberries, hull and slice them. Leave smaller berries whole.

Cook the Berries:
- In a saucepan, combine the mixed berries, sugar, and lemon juice.
- Heat the mixture over medium heat, stirring gently to combine. Allow the berries to release their juices and the sugar to dissolve.

Thicken the Compote (Optional):
- If you prefer a thicker consistency, mix cornstarch with a little water to make a slurry. Stir the slurry into the berry mixture.
- Continue to cook, stirring frequently until the compote thickens slightly. This should only take a few minutes.

Simmer and Mash (Optional):
- Let the compote simmer for a few more minutes. If you like a smoother consistency, you can use a fork or a potato masher to gently mash some of the berries.

Adjust Sweetness:
- Taste the compote and adjust the sweetness by adding more sugar if needed.

Cool and Serve:
- Allow the berry compote to cool to room temperature.
- Serve it over pancakes, waffles, ice cream, yogurt, cheesecake, or any dessert of your choice.

Enjoy this simple and versatile berry compote that adds a burst of fruity goodness to your favorite dishes!

Slow Cooker Tiramisu

Ingredients:

For the Pudding:

- 1 package (3.4 oz) instant vanilla pudding mix
- 2 cups cold milk
- 1 cup strong brewed coffee, cooled
- 1/4 cup coffee liqueur (optional)
- 1 package ladyfingers (about 24)

For the Topping:

- 1 cup heavy cream
- 2 tablespoons powdered sugar
- Cocoa powder, for dusting

Instructions:

Prepare the Pudding:
- In a bowl, whisk together the instant vanilla pudding mix and cold milk until well combined. Let it set according to package instructions.

Prepare the Coffee Mixture:
- In a shallow dish, combine the brewed coffee and coffee liqueur (if using).

Assemble the Layers:
- Dip each ladyfinger into the coffee mixture briefly, ensuring they are soaked but not overly soggy.
- Place a layer of soaked ladyfingers at the bottom of the slow cooker.
- Spread half of the prepared pudding over the ladyfingers.
- Repeat the layering with another layer of soaked ladyfingers and the remaining pudding.

Chill:
- Cover the slow cooker and refrigerate for at least 4 hours or overnight to allow the flavors to meld.

Prepare the Topping:
- Before serving, whip the heavy cream and powdered sugar until stiff peaks form.

Serve:

- Spoon the whipped cream over the chilled tiramisu.
- Dust the top with cocoa powder for a finishing touch.

Enjoy:
- Serve the slow cooker tiramisu in individual portions.

While this slow cooker version simplifies the process, it captures the essence of tiramisu with layers of coffee-soaked ladyfingers and creamy pudding.

Pumpkin Spice Latte

Ingredients:

- 1 cup milk (whole milk or your choice of plant-based milk)
- 1 tablespoon canned pumpkin puree
- 1-2 tablespoons granulated sugar (adjust to taste)
- 1/2 teaspoon pumpkin pie spice (plus extra for garnish)
- 1/2 teaspoon vanilla extract
- 1/2 cup strong brewed coffee or 1-2 shots of espresso
- Whipped cream (optional, for topping)

Instructions:

Prepare Coffee:
- Brew a strong cup of coffee or make 1-2 shots of espresso.

Heat Milk Mixture:
- In a small saucepan, heat the milk, pumpkin puree, and sugar over medium heat. Whisk continuously until the mixture is hot but not boiling.

Add Pumpkin Spice and Vanilla:
- Stir in the pumpkin pie spice and vanilla extract. Continue to whisk until the mixture is well combined and heated through.

Froth the Milk (Optional):
- Use a milk frother to froth the milk mixture for a creamy texture. If you don't have a frother, you can skip this step.

Combine Coffee and Pumpkin Milk:
- Pour the brewed coffee or espresso into your mug.
- Slowly pour the pumpkin spiced milk over the coffee.

Top with Whipped Cream and Spice:
- If desired, top the latte with whipped cream and sprinkle a little extra pumpkin pie spice on top.

Enjoy:
- Stir everything together and savor your homemade Pumpkin Spice Latte.

Now you can enjoy the flavors of fall with a cozy and delicious Pumpkin Spice Latte right at home!

Chicken Creations:

Chicken Curry

Ingredients:

- 1.5 lbs (about 700g) boneless, skinless chicken thighs, cut into bite-sized pieces
- 2 tablespoons vegetable oil
- 1 large onion, finely chopped
- 3 cloves garlic, minced
- 1 tablespoon ginger, grated
- 2 tablespoons curry powder
- 1 teaspoon ground turmeric
- 1 teaspoon ground cumin
- 1 teaspoon chili powder (adjust to taste)
- 1 can (14 oz) diced tomatoes
- 1 can (14 oz) coconut milk
- Salt and pepper to taste
- Fresh cilantro, chopped (for garnish)
- Cooked rice or naan bread (for serving)

Instructions:

Prepare the Chicken:
- Season the chicken pieces with salt and pepper.

Sear the Chicken:
- In a large skillet or pot, heat the vegetable oil over medium-high heat. Add the chicken pieces and brown them on all sides. Once browned, transfer the chicken to a plate and set aside.

Sauté Aromatics:
- In the same skillet, add chopped onions and sauté until softened.
- Add minced garlic and grated ginger, and sauté for an additional 1-2 minutes until fragrant.

Add Spices:
- Sprinkle curry powder, ground turmeric, ground cumin, and chili powder over the onions. Stir well to coat the onions in the spices.

Combine with Tomatoes and Coconut Milk:
- Pour in the diced tomatoes with their juices and coconut milk. Stir to combine.

Simmer:

- Bring the mixture to a simmer, then add back the seared chicken. Reduce the heat to low, cover, and let it simmer for about 20-25 minutes, or until the chicken is cooked through and tender.

Adjust Seasoning:
- Taste the curry and adjust the seasoning with salt and pepper as needed.

Serve:
- Serve the chicken curry over cooked rice or with naan bread.

Garnish:
- Garnish with chopped cilantro before serving.

Enjoy your homemade Chicken Curry with its flavorful and aromatic blend of spices!

Lemon Garlic Chicken Thighs

Ingredients:

- 4-6 bone-in, skin-on chicken thighs
- Salt and black pepper to taste
- 2 tablespoons olive oil
- 4 cloves garlic, minced
- 1 teaspoon dried thyme
- 1 teaspoon dried rosemary
- Zest of 1 lemon
- Juice of 1 lemon
- 1/2 cup chicken broth
- Fresh parsley, chopped (for garnish)

Instructions:

Preheat the Oven:
- Preheat your oven to 400°F (200°C).

Season Chicken Thighs:
- Pat the chicken thighs dry with paper towels. Season them with salt and black pepper on both sides.

Sear Chicken Thighs:
- In an oven-safe skillet, heat olive oil over medium-high heat. Add chicken thighs, skin side down, and sear until golden brown, about 4-5 minutes per side. Remove excess rendered fat if needed.

Sauté Garlic and Herbs:
- Lower the heat to medium, add minced garlic, dried thyme, and dried rosemary to the skillet. Sauté for about 1-2 minutes until fragrant.

Add Lemon Zest and Juice:
- Stir in the lemon zest and lemon juice. Make sure to scrape any browned bits from the bottom of the skillet for added flavor.

Pour in Chicken Broth:
- Pour in the chicken broth around the chicken thighs.

Bake in the Oven:
- Transfer the skillet to the preheated oven. Bake for about 25-30 minutes or until the chicken reaches an internal temperature of 165°F (74°C) and the skin is crispy.

Garnish and Serve:
- Remove the skillet from the oven, and garnish the chicken thighs with chopped fresh parsley.

Serve:
- Serve the lemon garlic chicken thighs over rice, pasta, or with your favorite side dishes.

This Lemon Garlic Chicken Thighs recipe delivers a delicious and juicy result with a perfect blend of citrus and herbs. Enjoy your meal!

Buffalo Chicken Dip

Ingredients:

- 2 cups cooked and shredded chicken (rotisserie chicken works well)
- 8 oz (about 1 cup) cream cheese, softened
- 1/2 cup mayonnaise
- 1/2 cup sour cream
- 1 cup shredded cheddar cheese
- 1/2 cup buffalo sauce (adjust to taste)
- 1 teaspoon garlic powder
- 1 teaspoon onion powder
- 1/2 teaspoon dried dill (optional)
- Salt and pepper to taste
- Green onions, chopped (for garnish)
- Celery sticks or tortilla chips (for serving)

Instructions:

Preheat Oven:
- Preheat your oven to 375°F (190°C).

Combine Ingredients:
- In a large mixing bowl, combine the shredded chicken, softened cream cheese, mayonnaise, sour cream, shredded cheddar cheese, buffalo sauce, garlic powder, onion powder, dried dill (if using), salt, and pepper. Mix until well combined.

Transfer to Baking Dish:
- Transfer the mixture to a baking dish, spreading it out evenly.

Bake:
- Bake in the preheated oven for 25-30 minutes, or until the dip is hot and bubbly, and the top is golden brown.

Garnish and Serve:
- Remove from the oven and garnish with chopped green onions.

Serve:
- Serve the Buffalo Chicken Dip warm with celery sticks, tortilla chips, or your favorite dipping options.

This Buffalo Chicken Dip is perfect for parties, game days, or any gathering where you want a delicious and satisfying appetizer. Enjoy!

Chicken Alfredo Pasta

Ingredients:

- 8 oz (about 225g) fettuccine pasta
- 2 tablespoons unsalted butter
- 1 lb (about 450g) boneless, skinless chicken breasts, cut into bite-sized pieces
- Salt and black pepper to taste
- 3 cloves garlic, minced
- 1 cup heavy cream
- 1 cup grated Parmesan cheese
- 1/2 cup unsalted chicken broth
- 1 teaspoon garlic powder
- 1 teaspoon onion powder
- 1 teaspoon dried Italian seasoning (optional)
- Fresh parsley, chopped (for garnish)

Instructions:

Cook the Pasta:
- Cook the fettuccine pasta according to the package instructions in a large pot of salted boiling water. Drain and set aside.

Cook the Chicken:
- In a large skillet, melt the butter over medium-high heat. Season the chicken pieces with salt and black pepper.
- Add the chicken to the skillet and cook until browned and cooked through, about 5-6 minutes. Remove the chicken from the skillet and set aside.

Sauté Garlic:
- In the same skillet, add minced garlic and sauté for about 1 minute until fragrant.

Prepare the Alfredo Sauce:
- Pour in the heavy cream, chicken broth, and grated Parmesan cheese. Stir continuously until the cheese is melted and the sauce is smooth.
- Season the sauce with garlic powder, onion powder, and dried Italian seasoning (if using).

Combine Chicken and Pasta:
- Add the cooked chicken back to the skillet, stirring to coat the chicken in the Alfredo sauce.

Add Pasta:

- Add the cooked fettuccine pasta to the skillet, tossing to combine and coat the pasta in the creamy sauce.

Serve:
- Garnish with chopped fresh parsley.

Enjoy:
- Serve the Chicken Alfredo Pasta hot, and enjoy your creamy and delicious homemade dish.

This Chicken Alfredo Pasta is a comforting and satisfying meal that's perfect for a family dinner or special occasion. Enjoy!

Honey Mustard Chicken

Ingredients:

- 4 boneless, skinless chicken breasts
- Salt and black pepper to taste
- 2 tablespoons olive oil
- 1/4 cup Dijon mustard
- 2 tablespoons whole grain mustard
- 3 tablespoons honey
- 2 cloves garlic, minced
- 1 teaspoon dried thyme (or 1 tablespoon fresh thyme)
- 1/2 cup chicken broth
- Fresh parsley, chopped (for garnish)

Instructions:

Season Chicken:
- Season the chicken breasts with salt and black pepper on both sides.

Sear Chicken:
- In a large skillet, heat olive oil over medium-high heat. Add the chicken breasts and sear until golden brown on both sides, about 3-4 minutes per side. Remove chicken from the skillet and set aside.

Prepare Honey Mustard Sauce:
- In the same skillet, add Dijon mustard, whole grain mustard, honey, minced garlic, and dried thyme. Stir to combine.

Add Chicken Broth:
- Pour in the chicken broth, stirring to create a smooth sauce.

Simmer:
- Return the seared chicken breasts to the skillet, coating them in the honey mustard sauce. Allow the chicken to simmer in the sauce for 10-12 minutes, or until the chicken is cooked through and reaches an internal temperature of 165°F (74°C).

Check Seasoning:
- Taste the sauce and adjust the seasoning, adding more salt or pepper if needed.

Serve:
- Garnish with chopped fresh parsley.

Enjoy:
- Serve the Honey Mustard Chicken hot, drizzling extra sauce over the top.

This Honey Mustard Chicken is a flavorful and versatile dish that pairs well with rice, potatoes, or your favorite side vegetables. Enjoy your delicious meal!

Coq au Vin

Ingredients:

- 1 whole chicken (about 3-4 pounds), cut into pieces
- Salt and black pepper to taste
- 2 tablespoons olive oil
- 4 ounces bacon, diced
- 8 ounces pearl onions, peeled
- 2 cloves garlic, minced
- 1 pound mushrooms, sliced
- 2 tablespoons all-purpose flour
- 1 bottle (750 ml) red wine (such as Burgundy or Pinot Noir)
- 1 cup chicken broth
- 2 tablespoons tomato paste
- 1 teaspoon dried thyme
- 2 bay leaves
- Fresh parsley, chopped (for garnish)

Instructions:

Season and Brown Chicken:
- Season the chicken pieces with salt and black pepper. In a large Dutch oven or heavy pot, heat olive oil over medium-high heat. Brown the chicken pieces on all sides. Remove the chicken and set aside.

Cook Bacon and Vegetables:
- In the same pot, add diced bacon and cook until it becomes crispy. Add pearl onions, minced garlic, and sliced mushrooms. Cook until the vegetables are slightly softened.

Add Flour:
- Sprinkle flour over the vegetables and bacon, stirring to coat. Cook for 1-2 minutes to eliminate the raw flour taste.

Deglaze with Wine:
- Pour in the red wine to deglaze the pot, scraping up any browned bits from the bottom. Allow the wine to simmer for a few minutes.

Add Chicken and Broth:
- Return the browned chicken to the pot. Add chicken broth, tomato paste, dried thyme, and bay leaves. Bring the mixture to a simmer.

Simmer and Cook:
- Reduce the heat to low, cover the pot, and let it simmer for about 1.5 to 2 hours, or until the chicken is tender and cooked through.

Check Seasoning and Garnish:
- Check and adjust the seasoning if needed. Remove bay leaves. Garnish with chopped fresh parsley.

Serve:
- Serve Coq au Vin over mashed potatoes, noodles, or crusty bread.

Coq au Vin is a comforting and rich dish that's perfect for special occasions or when you want to impress with a classic French meal. Enjoy!

Chicken and Dumplings

Ingredients:

For the Chicken Stew:

- 1 whole chicken (about 3-4 pounds), cut into pieces
- Salt and black pepper to taste
- 2 tablespoons vegetable oil
- 1 large onion, chopped
- 3 carrots, peeled and sliced
- 3 celery stalks, sliced
- 4 cloves garlic, minced
- 1/4 cup all-purpose flour
- 6 cups chicken broth
- 1 teaspoon dried thyme
- 2 bay leaves
- 1 cup frozen peas (optional)
- Fresh parsley, chopped (for garnish)

For the Dumplings:

- 2 cups all-purpose flour
- 1 tablespoon baking powder
- 1/2 teaspoon salt
- 3/4 cup milk
- 1/3 cup unsalted butter, melted

Instructions:

For the Chicken Stew:

Season and Brown Chicken:
- Season the chicken pieces with salt and black pepper. In a large pot or Dutch oven, heat vegetable oil over medium-high heat. Brown the chicken pieces on all sides. Remove the chicken and set aside.

Sauté Vegetables:

- In the same pot, add chopped onion, carrots, celery, and minced garlic. Sauté until the vegetables are softened.

Add Flour:
- Sprinkle flour over the vegetables, stirring to coat. Cook for 1-2 minutes.

Add Chicken and Broth:
- Return the browned chicken to the pot. Pour in the chicken broth, add dried thyme, and add bay leaves. Bring to a simmer.

Simmer:
- Cover the pot and let it simmer for about 45 minutes to 1 hour, or until the chicken is cooked through and tender.

Remove Chicken and Shred:
- Remove the chicken from the pot and shred the meat using two forks. Discard bones and skin.

Add Peas (Optional) and Shredded Chicken:
- If using peas, add them to the pot. Return the shredded chicken to the pot. Simmer for an additional 10 minutes.

Check Seasoning and Garnish:
- Check and adjust the seasoning. Remove bay leaves. Garnish with chopped fresh parsley.

For the Dumplings:

Prepare Dumpling Dough:
- In a mixing bowl, whisk together flour, baking powder, and salt. Add milk and melted butter, stirring until just combined. Do not overmix.

Drop Dumplings:
- Drop spoonfuls of the dumpling dough onto the simmering chicken stew. Cover the pot and let the dumplings cook for about 15 minutes, or until they are cooked through and fluffy.

Serve:
- Serve the Chicken and Dumplings hot, ladling the stew and dumplings into bowls.

This Chicken and Dumplings recipe brings together a rich, flavorful stew with fluffy dumplings for a comforting and satisfying meal. Enjoy!

Chicken Fajitas

Ingredients:

For the Chicken Marinade:

- 1.5 lbs (about 700g) boneless, skinless chicken breasts, thinly sliced
- 3 tablespoons olive oil
- 3 tablespoons lime juice
- 2 cloves garlic, minced
- 1 teaspoon chili powder
- 1 teaspoon ground cumin
- 1 teaspoon paprika
- 1 teaspoon onion powder
- 1/2 teaspoon dried oregano
- Salt and black pepper to taste

For the Fajitas:

- 2 bell peppers, thinly sliced (use a mix of colors)
- 1 large onion, thinly sliced
- 2 tablespoons vegetable oil
- Flour tortillas
- Optional toppings: salsa, guacamole, sour cream, shredded cheese, chopped cilantro, lime wedges

Instructions:

Marinate the Chicken:
- In a bowl, combine olive oil, lime juice, minced garlic, chili powder, ground cumin, paprika, onion powder, dried oregano, salt, and black pepper. Add sliced chicken to the marinade, ensuring each piece is coated. Let it marinate for at least 30 minutes, or refrigerate for up to 4 hours.

Cook the Chicken:
- Heat a large skillet or grill pan over medium-high heat. Add a bit of oil to the pan. Cook the marinated chicken slices until they are cooked through and have a nice char, about 4-5 minutes per side. Remove chicken from the pan and set aside.

Sauté Vegetables:

- In the same pan, add more oil if needed. Sauté the sliced bell peppers and onions until they are tender-crisp and slightly charred, about 5-7 minutes.

Combine Chicken and Vegetables:
- Return the cooked chicken to the pan with the sautéed vegetables. Toss everything together to combine and heat through.

Warm Tortillas:
- Heat the flour tortillas in a dry skillet or microwave until warm and pliable.

Assemble Fajitas:
- Spoon the chicken and vegetable mixture onto the warm tortillas.

Add Toppings:
- Top the fajitas with your favorite toppings such as salsa, guacamole, sour cream, shredded cheese, chopped cilantro, and a squeeze of lime juice.

Serve:
- Serve the Chicken Fajitas immediately, and enjoy!

These Chicken Fajitas make for a delicious and customizable meal, perfect for a quick and satisfying dinner.

Lemon Herb Chicken and Potatoes

Ingredients:

- 4 bone-in, skin-on chicken thighs
- 1.5 lbs (about 700g) baby potatoes, halved or quartered
- 3 tablespoons olive oil
- 4 cloves garlic, minced
- 1 lemon, sliced
- 1 teaspoon dried thyme
- 1 teaspoon dried rosemary
- 1 teaspoon dried oregano
- Salt and black pepper to taste
- Fresh parsley, chopped (for garnish)

Instructions:

Preheat Oven:
- Preheat your oven to 400°F (200°C).

Season Chicken and Potatoes:
- Pat the chicken thighs dry with paper towels. Season them with salt, black pepper, dried thyme, dried rosemary, and dried oregano. In a large bowl, toss the halved or quartered baby potatoes with olive oil, minced garlic, salt, and black pepper.

Arrange in Baking Dish:
- Place the seasoned chicken thighs and potatoes in a baking dish or on a baking sheet, arranging them in a single layer.

Add Lemon Slices:
- Scatter lemon slices over the chicken and potatoes.

Bake:
- Bake in the preheated oven for about 35-40 minutes or until the chicken is cooked through, and the potatoes are golden and tender.

Check Chicken and Potatoes:
- Check the chicken's internal temperature, which should reach 165°F (74°C). If the potatoes need more browning, you can broil for a few minutes.

Garnish:
- Garnish with chopped fresh parsley.

Serve:

- Serve the Lemon Herb Chicken and Potatoes hot, with lemon slices and pan juices.

This Lemon Herb Chicken and Potatoes dish is not only delicious but also requires minimal effort, making it a perfect option for a tasty and hassle-free dinner. Enjoy!

Chicken Tikka Masala

Ingredients:

For the Chicken Marinade:

- 1.5 lbs (about 700g) boneless, skinless chicken thighs or breasts, cut into bite-sized pieces
- 1 cup plain yogurt
- 2 tablespoons ginger-garlic paste
- 1 teaspoon ground turmeric
- 1 teaspoon ground cumin
- 1 teaspoon ground coriander
- 1 teaspoon chili powder (adjust to taste)
- Salt and black pepper to taste
- 2 tablespoons vegetable oil

For the Sauce:

- 2 tablespoons vegetable oil
- 1 large onion, finely chopped
- 4 cloves garlic, minced
- 1 tablespoon ginger, grated
- 1 teaspoon ground turmeric
- 2 teaspoons ground cumin
- 2 teaspoons ground coriander
- 2 teaspoons smoked paprika
- 1 teaspoon chili powder (adjust to taste)
- 1 can (14 oz) crushed tomatoes
- 1 cup heavy cream
- Salt and black pepper to taste
- Fresh cilantro, chopped (for garnish)
- Cooked basmati rice or naan bread (for serving)

Instructions:

For the Chicken Marinade:

    Marinate Chicken:

- In a bowl, mix together yogurt, ginger-garlic paste, ground turmeric, ground cumin, ground coriander, chili powder, salt, black pepper, and vegetable oil. Add chicken pieces, ensuring they are well-coated. Marinate for at least 1 hour, or overnight for best results.

Cook Chicken:
- Preheat the oven to 400°F (200°C). Thread marinated chicken pieces onto skewers and place them on a baking sheet. Bake for about 20-25 minutes or until the chicken is cooked through and has a nice char.

For the Sauce:

Sauté Aromatics:
- In a large skillet or pot, heat vegetable oil over medium heat. Add chopped onion and sauté until softened.

Add Spices:
- Add minced garlic, grated ginger, ground turmeric, ground cumin, ground coriander, smoked paprika, and chili powder. Stir well and cook for 1-2 minutes until fragrant.

Combine Tomatoes and Cream:
- Pour in crushed tomatoes and heavy cream. Stir to combine. Bring the mixture to a simmer and let it cook for 15-20 minutes, allowing the flavors to meld. Season with salt and black pepper to taste.

Blend Sauce (Optional):
- For a smoother texture, you can use an immersion blender to blend the sauce until smooth. Alternatively, leave it chunky if you prefer.

Add Cooked Chicken:
- Add the baked chicken pieces to the sauce. Simmer for an additional 10-15 minutes.

Garnish and Serve:
- Garnish with chopped fresh cilantro. Serve Chicken Tikka Masala hot over cooked basmati rice or with naan bread.

Enjoy this delicious and authentic Chicken Tikka Masala with its rich and creamy curry sauce!

Balsamic Glazed Chicken

Ingredients:

- 4 boneless, skinless chicken breasts
- Salt and black pepper to taste
- 2 tablespoons olive oil
- 1/2 cup balsamic vinegar
- 1/4 cup honey
- 2 cloves garlic, minced
- 1 teaspoon dried thyme (or 1 tablespoon fresh thyme)
- 1 teaspoon dried rosemary (or 1 tablespoon fresh rosemary)
- 1 tablespoon Dijon mustard
- Fresh parsley, chopped (for garnish)

Instructions:

Preheat Oven:
- Preheat your oven to 400°F (200°C).

Season Chicken:
- Season the chicken breasts with salt and black pepper on both sides.

Sear Chicken:
- In an oven-safe skillet, heat olive oil over medium-high heat. Add the chicken breasts and sear until golden brown on both sides, about 2-3 minutes per side. Remove chicken from the skillet and set aside.

Prepare Glaze:
- In the same skillet, add balsamic vinegar, honey, minced garlic, dried thyme, dried rosemary, and Dijon mustard. Stir to combine.

Simmer and Glaze:
- Allow the glaze to simmer and thicken for 2-3 minutes. Return the seared chicken to the skillet, coating each piece in the balsamic glaze.

Bake:
- Transfer the skillet to the preheated oven. Bake for about 15-20 minutes or until the chicken is cooked through, and the glaze has caramelized.

Check Doneness:
- Check the internal temperature of the chicken, which should reach 165°F (74°C).

Garnish and Serve:

- Garnish with chopped fresh parsley. Serve the Balsamic Glazed Chicken hot.

This Balsamic Glazed Chicken is a delicious and elegant dish that pairs well with a variety of sides, such as roasted vegetables, mashed potatoes, or a simple salad. Enjoy your meal!

Slow Cooker Chicken Marsala

Ingredients:

- 4 boneless, skinless chicken breasts
- Salt and black pepper to taste
- 1 cup all-purpose flour (for dredging)
- 2 tablespoons olive oil
- 8 oz (about 225g) mushrooms, sliced
- 3/4 cup Marsala wine
- 3/4 cup chicken broth
- 2 tablespoons unsalted butter
- 2 tablespoons fresh parsley, chopped (for garnish)

Instructions:

Season and Dredge Chicken:
- Season the chicken breasts with salt and black pepper. Dredge each chicken breast in flour, shaking off excess.

Sear Chicken:
- In a large skillet, heat olive oil over medium-high heat. Add the chicken breasts and sear until golden brown on both sides, about 3-4 minutes per side. Transfer the seared chicken to the slow cooker.

Sauté Mushrooms:
- In the same skillet, add sliced mushrooms and cook until they release their moisture and become golden brown.

Add Marsala Wine and Chicken Broth:
- Pour Marsala wine and chicken broth into the skillet, scraping up any browned bits from the bottom. Bring the mixture to a simmer.

Transfer to Slow Cooker:
- Pour the mushroom and Marsala mixture over the chicken in the slow cooker.

Cook in Slow Cooker:
- Cover the slow cooker and cook on low for 4-5 hours or until the chicken is cooked through and tender.

Finish with Butter:
- In the last 30 minutes of cooking, add unsalted butter to the slow cooker, allowing it to melt into the sauce.

Garnish and Serve:

- Garnish with chopped fresh parsley. Serve the Slow Cooker Chicken Marsala over cooked pasta, rice, or mashed potatoes.

This Slow Cooker Chicken Marsala is a convenient way to enjoy the rich and savory flavors of the classic dish with minimal effort. Enjoy your delicious meal!

Greek Chicken Gyros

Ingredients:

For the Greek Chicken:

- 1.5 lbs (about 700g) boneless, skinless chicken thighs, thinly sliced
- 3 tablespoons olive oil
- 3 cloves garlic, minced
- 1 tablespoon dried oregano
- 1 teaspoon ground cumin
- 1 teaspoon smoked paprika
- Salt and black pepper to taste
- Juice of 1 lemon

For Tzatziki Sauce:

- 1 cup Greek yogurt
- 1 cucumber, finely diced
- 2 cloves garlic, minced
- 1 tablespoon fresh dill, chopped
- 1 tablespoon olive oil
- Salt and black pepper to taste

For Assembling Gyros:

- Pita bread or flatbreads
- Sliced tomatoes
- Sliced cucumbers
- Red onion, thinly sliced
- Fresh lettuce or spinach
- Feta cheese, crumbled (optional)
- Kalamata olives (optional)

Instructions:

For Greek Chicken:

    Marinate Chicken:

- In a bowl, combine olive oil, minced garlic, dried oregano, ground cumin, smoked paprika, salt, black pepper, and lemon juice. Add sliced chicken thighs and marinate for at least 30 minutes, or refrigerate for up to 4 hours.

Cook Chicken:
- Heat a skillet or grill pan over medium-high heat. Cook the marinated chicken slices until fully cooked and have a nice char, about 4-5 minutes per side.

For Tzatziki Sauce:

Prepare Tzatziki:
- In a bowl, mix together Greek yogurt, finely diced cucumber, minced garlic, chopped fresh dill, olive oil, salt, and black pepper. Adjust seasoning to taste.

For Assembling Gyros:

Warm Pita Bread:
- Warm the pita bread or flatbreads in a dry skillet or microwave.

Assemble Gyros:
- Spread a generous spoonful of tzatziki sauce onto each pita bread. Add sliced Greek chicken on top. Layer with sliced tomatoes, cucumbers, red onion, lettuce or spinach, crumbled feta cheese, and Kalamata olives.

Fold and Serve:
- Fold the gyros and secure with toothpicks if needed. Serve immediately.

These homemade Greek Chicken Gyros are a delicious and healthier alternative to takeout. Customize with your favorite toppings and enjoy a taste of Greece!

Cranberry Orange Chicken

Ingredients:

- 4 boneless, skinless chicken breasts
- Salt and black pepper to taste
- 2 tablespoons olive oil
- 1 cup cranberry sauce (homemade or store-bought)
- 1/2 cup orange juice
- Zest of 1 orange
- 2 tablespoons soy sauce
- 1 tablespoon Dijon mustard
- 2 cloves garlic, minced
- 1 teaspoon dried thyme (or 1 tablespoon fresh thyme)
- 1 tablespoon cornstarch (optional, for thickening)
- Fresh parsley, chopped (for garnish)

Instructions:

Season Chicken:
- Season the chicken breasts with salt and black pepper on both sides.

Sear Chicken:
- In a large skillet, heat olive oil over medium-high heat. Add the seasoned chicken breasts and sear until golden brown on both sides. Remove the chicken from the skillet and set aside.

Prepare Sauce:
- In the same skillet, add cranberry sauce, orange juice, orange zest, soy sauce, Dijon mustard, minced garlic, and dried thyme. Stir to combine.

Cook Chicken in Sauce:
- Return the seared chicken to the skillet, coating each piece in the cranberry-orange sauce. Simmer for 15-20 minutes or until the chicken is cooked through and the sauce has thickened.

Check Doneness:
- Check the internal temperature of the chicken, which should reach 165°F (74°C).

Thicken Sauce (Optional):

- If you desire a thicker sauce, mix cornstarch with a tablespoon of water to create a slurry. Stir it into the sauce and let it simmer for an additional 2-3 minutes until thickened.

Garnish and Serve:
- Garnish with chopped fresh parsley. Serve the Cranberry Orange Chicken over cooked rice or with your favorite side dishes.

This Cranberry Orange Chicken is a delightful combination of flavors that is perfect for a festive meal. Enjoy the sweet and tangy goodness!

Cajun Chicken and Sausage Jambalaya

Ingredients:

- 1 lb (about 450g) boneless, skinless chicken thighs, cut into bite-sized pieces
- 1/2 lb (about 225g) andouille sausage, sliced
- 1 large onion, diced
- 1 bell pepper, diced
- 2 celery stalks, diced
- 3 cloves garlic, minced
- 1 cup long-grain white rice
- 1 can (14 oz) diced tomatoes, undrained
- 2 cups chicken broth
- 1 teaspoon Cajun seasoning
- 1 teaspoon dried thyme
- 1 teaspoon paprika
- 1/2 teaspoon dried oregano
- 1/2 teaspoon cayenne pepper (adjust to taste)
- Salt and black pepper to taste
- Green onions, sliced (for garnish)
- Fresh parsley, chopped (for garnish)

Instructions:

Season Chicken:
- Season the chicken pieces with Cajun seasoning, paprika, dried thyme, dried oregano, cayenne pepper, salt, and black pepper.

Sear Chicken and Sausage:
- In a large, deep skillet or Dutch oven, heat a bit of oil over medium-high heat. Add the seasoned chicken and sliced andouille sausage. Sear until the chicken is browned on all sides. Remove chicken and sausage from the skillet and set aside.

Sauté Vegetables:
- In the same skillet, add diced onion, bell pepper, celery, and minced garlic. Sauté until the vegetables are softened.

Add Rice and Tomatoes:
- Stir in the long-grain white rice and cook for 2-3 minutes. Add the diced tomatoes with their juices and stir to combine.

Combine Chicken and Sausage:

- Return the seared chicken and sausage to the skillet, mixing them with the vegetables and rice.

Add Chicken Broth:
- Pour in the chicken broth, stirring to combine. Bring the mixture to a simmer.

Simmer:
- Cover the skillet and let it simmer over medium-low heat for about 20-25 minutes or until the rice is cooked, and the liquid is absorbed. Stir occasionally.

Check Seasoning:
- Taste and adjust the seasoning if needed. Add more salt, pepper, or Cajun seasoning according to your preference.

Garnish and Serve:
- Garnish the Cajun Chicken and Sausage Jambalaya with sliced green onions and chopped fresh parsley. Serve hot.

This Cajun Chicken and Sausage Jambalaya is a comforting and flavorful dish that captures the essence of Cajun cuisine. Enjoy this one-pot wonder!

Hearty Soups and Chilis:
Black Bean Soup

Ingredients:

- 2 cans (15 oz each) black beans, drained and rinsed
- 1 tablespoon olive oil
- 1 onion, finely chopped
- 2 carrots, diced
- 2 celery stalks, diced
- 3 cloves garlic, minced
- 1 teaspoon ground cumin
- 1 teaspoon chili powder
- 1/2 teaspoon smoked paprika
- 4 cups vegetable or chicken broth
- 1 bay leaf
- Salt and black pepper to taste
- Juice of 1 lime
- Fresh cilantro, chopped (for garnish)
- Sour cream or Greek yogurt (optional, for serving)

Instructions:

Sauté Vegetables:
- In a large pot, heat olive oil over medium heat. Add chopped onion, diced carrots, and diced celery. Sauté until the vegetables are softened, about 5-7 minutes.

Add Garlic and Spices:
- Add minced garlic, ground cumin, chili powder, and smoked paprika. Stir well and cook for an additional 1-2 minutes until the spices are fragrant.

Add Black Beans:
- Add the drained and rinsed black beans to the pot. Stir to combine with the sautéed vegetables and spices.

Pour in Broth:
- Pour in the vegetable or chicken broth. Add the bay leaf. Bring the mixture to a simmer.

Simmer:

- Reduce the heat to low, cover the pot, and let it simmer for about 20-25 minutes to allow the flavors to meld.

Season and Blend (Optional):
- Season the soup with salt and black pepper to taste. If you prefer a smoother texture, you can use an immersion blender to partially blend the soup.

Finish with Lime Juice:
- Squeeze the juice of one lime into the soup. Stir to combine.

Serve:
- Ladle the Black Bean Soup into bowls. Garnish with chopped fresh cilantro. Optionally, add a dollop of sour cream or Greek yogurt on top.

This Black Bean Soup is delicious, nutritious, and can be customized with your favorite toppings. Enjoy a warm and comforting bowl!

Tuscan White Bean Soup

Ingredients:

- 2 tablespoons olive oil
- 1 onion, finely chopped
- 2 carrots, diced
- 2 celery stalks, diced
- 3 cloves garlic, minced
- 2 teaspoons dried Italian herbs (blend of oregano, thyme, rosemary)
- 2 cans (15 oz each) cannellini beans, drained and rinsed
- 1 can (14 oz) diced tomatoes, undrained
- 4 cups vegetable or chicken broth
- 1 bunch kale, stems removed and leaves chopped
- Salt and black pepper to taste
- 1/2 cup grated Parmesan cheese (for garnish)
- Crusty bread (for serving)

Instructions:

Sauté Vegetables:
- In a large pot, heat olive oil over medium heat. Add chopped onion, diced carrots, and diced celery. Sauté until the vegetables are softened, about 5-7 minutes.

Add Garlic and Herbs:
- Add minced garlic and dried Italian herbs. Stir well and cook for an additional 1-2 minutes until the garlic is fragrant.

Add Beans and Tomatoes:
- Add the drained and rinsed cannellini beans and the undrained diced tomatoes to the pot. Stir to combine.

Pour in Broth:
- Pour in the vegetable or chicken broth. Bring the mixture to a simmer.

Cook Kale:
- Add the chopped kale to the pot. Simmer for about 10-15 minutes until the kale is tender.

Season:
- Season the soup with salt and black pepper to taste. Adjust the seasoning according to your preference.

Serve:

- Ladle the Tuscan White Bean Soup into bowls. Garnish with grated Parmesan cheese. Serve hot with crusty bread.

This Tuscan White Bean Soup is a nutritious and satisfying meal. The combination of beans, vegetables, and herbs creates a hearty and delicious flavor. Enjoy your comforting bowl of soup!

Mexican Chicken Tortilla Chili

Ingredients:

- 1 lb (about 450g) boneless, skinless chicken breasts, cooked and shredded
- 1 tablespoon olive oil
- 1 onion, finely chopped
- 3 cloves garlic, minced
- 1 bell pepper, diced
- 1 can (14 oz) diced tomatoes, undrained
- 1 can (15 oz) black beans, drained and rinsed
- 1 can (15 oz) kidney beans, drained and rinsed
- 1 can (15 oz) corn kernels, drained
- 1 can (4 oz) diced green chilies
- 1 can (10 oz) red enchilada sauce
- 1 tablespoon chili powder
- 1 teaspoon ground cumin
- 1 teaspoon smoked paprika
- Salt and black pepper to taste
- 4 cups chicken broth
- Tortilla chips, shredded cheese, avocado, and cilantro (for garnish)

Instructions:

Cook and Shred Chicken:
- Cook the chicken breasts by grilling, baking, or boiling. Shred the cooked chicken and set aside.

Sauté Vegetables:
- In a large pot, heat olive oil over medium heat. Add chopped onion, minced garlic, and diced bell pepper. Sauté until the vegetables are softened.

Add Tomatoes and Beans:
- Add diced tomatoes, black beans, kidney beans, corn kernels, and diced green chilies to the pot. Stir well.

Stir in Enchilada Sauce and Spices:
- Pour in the red enchilada sauce and add chili powder, ground cumin, smoked paprika, salt, and black pepper. Stir to combine.

Add Shredded Chicken:
- Incorporate the shredded chicken into the pot, mixing well with the other ingredients.

Pour in Chicken Broth:
- Add chicken broth to the pot. Bring the mixture to a simmer.

Simmer and Adjust Seasoning:
- Let the chili simmer for about 15-20 minutes to allow the flavors to meld. Taste and adjust the seasoning if needed.

Serve:
- Ladle the Mexican Chicken Tortilla Chili into bowls. Garnish with crushed tortilla chips, shredded cheese, sliced avocado, and chopped cilantro.

Enjoy this Mexican-inspired Chicken Tortilla Chili with a medley of toppings for a delicious and comforting meal!

Slow Cooker Lentil Chili

Ingredients:

- 1 cup dried brown lentils, rinsed and drained
- 1 can (15 oz) diced tomatoes, undrained
- 1 can (15 oz) tomato sauce
- 1 onion, finely chopped
- 3 cloves garlic, minced
- 1 bell pepper, diced
- 2 carrots, diced
- 2 celery stalks, diced
- 1 can (15 oz) black beans, drained and rinsed
- 1 can (15 oz) kidney beans, drained and rinsed
- 4 cups vegetable broth
- 2 tablespoons tomato paste
- 2 teaspoons ground cumin
- 2 teaspoons chili powder
- 1 teaspoon dried oregano
- 1 teaspoon smoked paprika
- 1/2 teaspoon ground coriander
- Salt and black pepper to taste
- Optional toppings: shredded cheese, sour cream, green onions, cilantro

Instructions:

Combine Ingredients in Slow Cooker:
- In a slow cooker, combine the brown lentils, diced tomatoes, tomato sauce, chopped onion, minced garlic, diced bell pepper, diced carrots, diced celery, black beans, kidney beans, vegetable broth, tomato paste, cumin, chili powder, oregano, smoked paprika, ground coriander, salt, and black pepper.

Stir Well:
- Stir all the ingredients in the slow cooker until well combined.

Cook on Low:
- Cover the slow cooker and cook on low for 6-8 hours or until the lentils are tender.

Adjust Seasoning:

- Taste the chili and adjust the seasoning if needed. Add more salt, pepper, or spices according to your preference.

Serve:
- Ladle the Slow Cooker Lentil Chili into bowls. Top with your favorite toppings such as shredded cheese, sour cream, green onions, or cilantro.

This Slow Cooker Lentil Chili is not only delicious but also a great option for a plant-based and protein-packed meal. Enjoy the warm and comforting flavors!

Moroccan Chickpea Stew

Ingredients:

- 2 tablespoons olive oil
- 1 onion, finely chopped
- 3 cloves garlic, minced
- 1 teaspoon ground cumin
- 1 teaspoon ground coriander
- 1 teaspoon smoked paprika
- 1 teaspoon ground turmeric
- 1/2 teaspoon ground cinnamon
- 1/2 teaspoon ground ginger
- 1/4 teaspoon cayenne pepper (adjust to taste)
- 1 can (15 oz) chickpeas, drained and rinsed
- 1 can (14 oz) diced tomatoes, undrained
- 2 carrots, peeled and diced
- 1 sweet potato, peeled and diced
- 4 cups vegetable broth
- 1 cup dried red lentils, rinsed and drained
- Salt and black pepper to taste
- 1 cup chopped spinach or kale
- Juice of 1 lemon
- Fresh cilantro, chopped (for garnish)
- Cooked couscous or rice (for serving)

Instructions:

Sauté Aromatics:
- In a large pot, heat olive oil over medium heat. Add chopped onion and sauté until softened.

Add Spices:
- Add minced garlic, ground cumin, ground coriander, smoked paprika, ground turmeric, ground cinnamon, ground ginger, and cayenne pepper. Stir well and cook for 1-2 minutes until fragrant.

Combine Chickpeas and Vegetables:
- Add chickpeas, diced tomatoes, diced carrots, diced sweet potato, vegetable broth, and red lentils to the pot. Stir to combine.

Simmer:
- Bring the stew to a simmer. Cover the pot and let it simmer for about 20-25 minutes or until the lentils and vegetables are tender.

Season and Add Greens:
- Season the stew with salt and black pepper to taste. Add chopped spinach or kale and stir until wilted.

Finish with Lemon Juice:
- Squeeze the juice of one lemon into the stew and stir to combine.

Serve:
- Ladle the Moroccan Chickpea Stew into bowls. Serve over cooked couscous or rice. Garnish with chopped fresh cilantro.

This Moroccan Chickpea Stew is rich in spices and flavors, making it a comforting and satisfying meal. Enjoy the exotic taste of Morocco!

Ham and Bean Soup

Ingredients:

- 1 cup dried navy beans, soaked overnight (or use canned beans for a quicker option)
- 1 tablespoon olive oil
- 1 onion, finely chopped
- 2 carrots, diced
- 2 celery stalks, diced
- 3 cloves garlic, minced
- 2 cups cooked ham, diced
- 6 cups chicken or vegetable broth
- 1 bay leaf
- 1 teaspoon dried thyme
- Salt and black pepper to taste
- 1 cup chopped kale or spinach (optional)
- Lemon wedges for serving

Instructions:

Prepare Beans (if using dried):
- If using dried beans, soak them overnight in water. Drain and rinse before using.

Sauté Vegetables:
- In a large pot, heat olive oil over medium heat. Add chopped onion, diced carrots, diced celery, and minced garlic. Sauté until the vegetables are softened.

Add Ham and Beans:
- Add diced ham and soaked (or canned) beans to the pot. Stir to combine.

Pour in Broth:
- Pour in the chicken or vegetable broth. Add the bay leaf and dried thyme. Bring the soup to a boil, then reduce the heat to low and simmer.

Simmer:
- Cover the pot and let the soup simmer for about 1 to 1.5 hours, or until the beans are tender. If using canned beans, simmer for about 30 minutes.

Season:
- Season the soup with salt and black pepper to taste. Remove the bay leaf.

Add Greens (Optional):
- Stir in chopped kale or spinach, if using, and cook for an additional 5 minutes until wilted.

Serve:
- Ladle the Ham and Bean Soup into bowls. Serve with lemon wedges on the side for a burst of freshness.

Enjoy this comforting and flavorful Ham and Bean Soup, perfect for a cozy meal, especially during colder weather!

Slow Cooker Sausage and Lentil Stew

Ingredients:

- 1 lb (about 450g) Italian sausage, casings removed
- 1 onion, finely chopped
- 2 carrots, diced
- 2 celery stalks, diced
- 3 cloves garlic, minced
- 1 cup dried green or brown lentils, rinsed and drained
- 1 can (14 oz) diced tomatoes, undrained
- 6 cups chicken or vegetable broth
- 1 teaspoon dried thyme
- 1 teaspoon dried rosemary
- 1 bay leaf
- Salt and black pepper to taste
- 2 cups chopped kale or spinach
- Fresh parsley, chopped (for garnish)

Instructions:

Brown Sausage:
- In a skillet over medium heat, brown the Italian sausage, breaking it into crumbles. Once browned, drain excess fat.

Combine Ingredients in Slow Cooker:
- In a slow cooker, combine the browned sausage, chopped onion, diced carrots, diced celery, minced garlic, rinsed lentils, diced tomatoes, chicken or vegetable broth, dried thyme, dried rosemary, and bay leaf.

Cook on Low:
- Cover the slow cooker and cook on low for 6-8 hours or until the lentils are tender.

Season:
- Season the stew with salt and black pepper to taste. Remove the bay leaf.

Add Greens:
- Stir in chopped kale or spinach during the last 30 minutes of cooking until wilted.

Serve:
- Ladle the Slow Cooker Sausage and Lentil Stew into bowls. Garnish with chopped fresh parsley.

This stew is not only delicious but also filling and nutritious, making it a perfect comfort food option. Enjoy your slow-cooked creation!

Vegetarian Taco Soup

Ingredients:

- 1 tablespoon olive oil
- 1 onion, diced
- 2 bell peppers (any color), diced
- 3 cloves garlic, minced
- 1 can (15 oz) black beans, drained and rinsed
- 1 can (15 oz) kidney beans, drained and rinsed
- 1 can (15 oz) corn kernels, drained
- 1 can (14 oz) diced tomatoes, undrained
- 1 can (4 oz) diced green chilies
- 4 cups vegetable broth
- 1 packet taco seasoning (or use homemade seasoning)
- Salt and black pepper to taste
- 1 cup cooked quinoa or rice
- Optional toppings: shredded cheese, sour cream, avocado, cilantro, lime wedges, tortilla chips

Instructions:

Sauté Vegetables:
- In a large pot, heat olive oil over medium heat. Add diced onion and bell peppers. Sauté until the vegetables are softened.

Add Garlic and Beans:
- Add minced garlic, black beans, kidney beans, and corn to the pot. Stir well.

Combine with Tomatoes and Broth:
- Add diced tomatoes with their juices, diced green chilies, vegetable broth, and taco seasoning to the pot. Stir to combine.

Simmer:
- Bring the soup to a simmer. Cover the pot and let it simmer for about 15-20 minutes to allow the flavors to meld.

Season:
- Season the soup with salt and black pepper to taste.

Add Cooked Quinoa or Rice:
- Stir in the cooked quinoa or rice. Simmer for an additional 5-10 minutes until the soup is heated through.

Serve:
- Ladle the Vegetarian Taco Soup into bowls. Top with your favorite toppings such as shredded cheese, sour cream, avocado slices, cilantro, and lime wedges. Serve with tortilla chips on the side.

Enjoy this Vegetarian Taco Soup for a delicious and comforting meal with all the flavors of tacos in a bowl!

Wild Rice and Mushroom Soup

Ingredients:

- 1 cup wild rice, uncooked
- 8 cups vegetable or chicken broth
- 3 tablespoons olive oil
- 1 onion, finely chopped
- 3 cloves garlic, minced
- 1 lb (about 450g) mushrooms, sliced (use a mix of varieties for depth of flavor)
- 2 carrots, diced
- 2 celery stalks, diced
- 1 teaspoon dried thyme
- 1 teaspoon dried rosemary
- 1/2 cup all-purpose flour
- 4 cups milk (whole or 2%)
- Salt and black pepper to taste
- 1/2 cup heavy cream (optional)
- Fresh parsley, chopped (for garnish)

Instructions:

Cook Wild Rice:
- In a separate pot, cook the wild rice according to package instructions. Drain and set aside.

Sauté Vegetables:
- In a large pot, heat olive oil over medium heat. Add chopped onion, minced garlic, sliced mushrooms, diced carrots, and diced celery. Sauté until the vegetables are softened.

Add Thyme and Rosemary:
- Stir in dried thyme and dried rosemary, cooking for an additional minute until fragrant.

Make Roux:
- Sprinkle flour over the vegetables and stir to create a roux. Cook for 2-3 minutes, allowing the flour to slightly brown.

Gradually Add Broth:
- Gradually add the vegetable or chicken broth, stirring constantly to avoid lumps. Bring the mixture to a simmer.

Simmer:

- Let the soup simmer for 15-20 minutes, allowing the vegetables to cook and the flavors to meld.

Add Cooked Wild Rice:
- Stir in the cooked wild rice and continue to simmer for an additional 10-15 minutes.

Pour in Milk:
- Pour in the milk, stirring continuously. Allow the soup to heat through without boiling.

Season:
- Season the soup with salt and black pepper to taste. Adjust the seasoning as needed.

Add Heavy Cream (Optional):
- If desired, add the heavy cream for extra richness. Stir to combine.

Serve:
- Ladle the Wild Rice and Mushroom Soup into bowls. Garnish with chopped fresh parsley.

This Wild Rice and Mushroom Soup is a comforting and hearty dish, perfect for cooler days. Enjoy the delicious combination of wild rice and mushrooms!

Thai Coconut Chicken Soup

Ingredients:

- 1 lb (about 450g) boneless, skinless chicken breasts, thinly sliced
- 1 can (14 oz) coconut milk
- 4 cups chicken broth
- 2 lemongrass stalks, bruised and chopped into 2-inch pieces
- 4-5 kaffir lime leaves, torn into pieces (optional)
- 3 tablespoons fish sauce
- 1 tablespoon soy sauce
- 1 tablespoon grated ginger
- 2 cloves garlic, minced
- 1-2 Thai bird's eye chilies, thinly sliced (adjust to taste)
- 8 oz mushrooms, sliced
- 1 medium-sized onion, thinly sliced
- 1 medium-sized tomato, diced
- 1 red bell pepper, thinly sliced
- 1 tablespoon vegetable oil
- Fresh cilantro leaves, chopped (for garnish)
- Lime wedges (for serving)
- Cooked jasmine rice (optional, for serving)

Instructions:

Prepare Lemongrass and Kaffir Lime Leaves:
- Bruise the lemongrass stalks by smashing them with the back of a knife. If using kaffir lime leaves, tear them into pieces.

Sauté Aromatics:
- In a large pot, heat vegetable oil over medium heat. Add minced garlic, grated ginger, and sliced Thai bird's eye chilies. Sauté for 1-2 minutes until fragrant.

Add Chicken:
- Add thinly sliced chicken to the pot. Cook until the chicken is no longer pink.

Pour in Coconut Milk and Broth:
- Pour in the coconut milk and chicken broth. Add the bruised lemongrass stalks and torn kaffir lime leaves. Bring the mixture to a simmer.

Season:

- Stir in fish sauce and soy sauce. Taste and adjust the seasoning as needed.

Add Vegetables:
- Add sliced mushrooms, thinly sliced onion, diced tomato, and sliced red bell pepper to the pot. Simmer for about 10-15 minutes until the vegetables are tender.

Discard Lemongrass and Lime Leaves:
- Before serving, remove the lemongrass stalks and torn kaffir lime leaves.

Serve:
- Ladle the Thai Coconut Chicken Soup into bowls. Garnish with chopped cilantro. Serve with lime wedges on the side.

Optional: Serve with Rice:
- If desired, serve the soup over cooked jasmine rice.

Enjoy this aromatic and creamy Thai Coconut Chicken Soup, filled with the vibrant flavors of Thai cuisine!

Sides and Dips:
Creamy Slow Cooker Mashed Potatoes

Ingredients:

- 5 lbs (about 2.3 kg) potatoes, peeled and diced
- 1 cup chicken or vegetable broth
- 1 cup milk (whole or 2%)
- 1/2 cup unsalted butter, cut into cubes
- Salt and black pepper to taste
- Optional toppings: chopped chives, grated cheese, additional butter

Instructions:

Prepare Potatoes:
- Peel and dice the potatoes into evenly sized chunks.

Cook Potatoes:
- Place the diced potatoes in the slow cooker. Pour in the chicken or vegetable broth.

Cook on High:
- Cover and cook on high for about 3-4 hours or until the potatoes are tender. The cooking time may vary depending on your slow cooker.

Mash Potatoes:
- Once the potatoes are tender, mash them directly in the slow cooker using a potato masher.

Add Butter and Milk:
- Add the cubed butter and pour in the milk. Continue mashing until the potatoes are smooth and creamy.

Season:
- Season the mashed potatoes with salt and black pepper to taste. Adjust the seasoning as needed.

Keep Warm:
- Reduce the slow cooker heat to low or warm to keep the mashed potatoes warm until serving.

Serve:
- Just before serving, give the mashed potatoes a final stir. Transfer to a serving bowl.

Garnish (Optional):

- If desired, garnish the creamy slow cooker mashed potatoes with chopped chives, grated cheese, or additional butter.

Enjoy these creamy and hassle-free slow cooker mashed potatoes at your next gathering or as a comforting side dish!

Slow Cooker Baked Beans

Ingredients:

- 1 lb (about 2 cups) dried navy beans, soaked overnight
- 1 onion, finely chopped
- 1/2 cup molasses
- 1/4 cup brown sugar
- 1/4 cup maple syrup
- 1/4 cup ketchup
- 2 tablespoons Dijon mustard
- 1 teaspoon salt
- 1/2 teaspoon black pepper
- 1/2 lb (about 225g) bacon, cooked and chopped (optional)
- 4 cups water or vegetable broth

Instructions:

Soak Beans:
- Rinse the dried navy beans and soak them overnight in water. Drain before using.

Combine Ingredients in Slow Cooker:
- In the slow cooker, combine the soaked navy beans, chopped onion, molasses, brown sugar, maple syrup, ketchup, Dijon mustard, salt, black pepper, and cooked and chopped bacon (if using).

Add Liquid:
- Pour in water or vegetable broth to cover the beans.

Cook on Low:
- Cover the slow cooker and cook on low for 6-8 hours or until the beans are tender.

Check Consistency:
- Check the consistency of the beans during cooking. If they are too dry, add more water or broth as needed.

Adjust Seasoning:
- Taste the baked beans and adjust the seasoning if necessary. Add more salt, pepper, or sweetness according to your preference.

Serve:
- Once the baked beans are tender and have absorbed the flavors, serve them hot.

Enjoy these delicious slow cooker baked beans as a side dish for barbecues, picnics, or any meal that calls for a comforting and hearty accompaniment!

Caramelized Onion Dip

Ingredients:

- 2 large onions, thinly sliced
- 2 tablespoons olive oil
- 1 cup sour cream
- 1/2 cup mayonnaise
- 1 teaspoon Worcestershire sauce
- 1/2 teaspoon garlic powder
- Salt and black pepper to taste
- Fresh chives or green onions, chopped (for garnish)
- Potato chips or vegetable sticks (for serving)

Instructions:

Caramelize Onions:
- In a skillet, heat olive oil over medium heat. Add thinly sliced onions and cook, stirring occasionally, until the onions are caramelized and golden brown. This may take about 20-30 minutes.

Prepare Dip Base:
- In a mixing bowl, combine sour cream, mayonnaise, Worcestershire sauce, garlic powder, salt, and black pepper.

Add Caramelized Onions:
- Once the onions are caramelized, allow them to cool slightly. Then, add the caramelized onions to the dip base. Stir well to combine.

Chill:
- Cover the bowl and refrigerate the caramelized onion dip for at least 1-2 hours to allow the flavors to meld.

Garnish:
- Before serving, garnish the dip with chopped fresh chives or green onions.

Serve:
- Serve the caramelized onion dip with potato chips or vegetable sticks.

This dip is perfect for parties, gatherings, or as a tasty snack. The rich and sweet flavor of caramelized onions adds a depth of flavor to the creamy dip. Enjoy!

Artichoke and Spinach Dip

Ingredients:

- 1 (10 oz) package frozen chopped spinach, thawed and drained
- 1 (14 oz) can artichoke hearts, drained and chopped
- 1 cup mayonnaise
- 1 cup sour cream
- 1 cup grated Parmesan cheese
- 1 cup shredded mozzarella cheese
- 1 teaspoon garlic powder
- 1/2 teaspoon onion powder
- Salt and black pepper to taste
- 1/2 cup shredded cheddar cheese (optional, for topping)
- Fresh parsley, chopped (for garnish)
- Tortilla chips, bread, or vegetable sticks (for serving)

Instructions:

Preheat Oven:
- Preheat your oven to 375°F (190°C).

Prepare Spinach and Artichokes:
- Make sure the frozen chopped spinach is thawed and well-drained. Chop the artichoke hearts into small pieces.

Mix Ingredients:
- In a large mixing bowl, combine the chopped spinach, chopped artichoke hearts, mayonnaise, sour cream, grated Parmesan cheese, shredded mozzarella cheese, garlic powder, onion powder, salt, and black pepper. Mix well.

Transfer to Baking Dish:
- Transfer the mixture to a baking dish, spreading it evenly.

Optional Topping:
- If desired, sprinkle shredded cheddar cheese on top for an extra layer of gooey goodness.

Bake:
- Bake in the preheated oven for about 25-30 minutes, or until the dip is hot and bubbly, and the top is golden brown.

Garnish:

- Remove from the oven and let it cool for a few minutes. Garnish with chopped fresh parsley.

Serve:
- Serve the Artichoke and Spinach Dip with tortilla chips, slices of bread, or vegetable sticks.

This warm and cheesy dip is a crowd-pleaser, perfect for parties and gatherings. Enjoy!

Slow Cooker Risotto

Ingredients:

- 1 1/2 cups Arborio rice
- 4 cups chicken or vegetable broth
- 1 cup dry white wine
- 1 small onion, finely chopped
- 2 cloves garlic, minced
- 1 cup grated Parmesan cheese
- 1/2 cup unsalted butter
- Salt and black pepper to taste
- Fresh herbs (such as parsley or thyme) for garnish (optional)

Instructions:

Prepare Ingredients:
- Chop the onion and garlic. Measure out the Arborio rice, chicken or vegetable broth, dry white wine, Parmesan cheese, and butter.

Combine Ingredients in Slow Cooker:
- In the slow cooker, combine Arborio rice, chopped onion, minced garlic, chicken or vegetable broth, and dry white wine. Stir well.

Cook on Low:
- Cover the slow cooker and cook on low for 2 to 2.5 hours. It's important not to overcook, as risotto can become mushy.

Stir in Butter and Parmesan:
- Once the rice is cooked and has absorbed most of the liquid, stir in the unsalted butter and grated Parmesan cheese. Mix until creamy and well combined.

Season:
- Season the risotto with salt and black pepper to taste. Adjust the seasoning if necessary.

Garnish:
- Optionally, garnish with fresh herbs like parsley or thyme.

Serve:
- Spoon the Slow Cooker Risotto onto plates or into bowls. Serve immediately, and enjoy the creamy goodness.

Note: The slow cooker method is not as traditional as cooking risotto on the stovetop, but it's a convenient and hands-free alternative.

Feel free to add cooked vegetables, sautéed mushrooms, or grilled chicken for added flavor and texture. Enjoy your slow-cooked risotto!

Garlic Parmesan Bread Pudding

Ingredients:

- 1 loaf of day-old French or Italian bread, cut into cubes (about 6-8 cups)
- 4 cups milk
- 4 large eggs
- 1 cup grated Parmesan cheese
- 1/2 cup unsalted butter, melted
- 4 cloves garlic, minced
- 2 teaspoons dried parsley
- 1 teaspoon dried thyme
- 1 teaspoon dried oregano
- 1/2 teaspoon salt
- 1/4 teaspoon black pepper
- Additional Parmesan for topping
- Fresh parsley, chopped (for garnish)

Instructions:

Preheat Oven:
- Preheat your oven to 350°F (175°C).

Prepare Bread Cubes:
- Cut the day-old bread into cubes and place them in a large mixing bowl.

Prepare Custard Mixture:
- In a separate bowl, whisk together the milk, eggs, grated Parmesan cheese, melted butter, minced garlic, dried parsley, dried thyme, dried oregano, salt, and black pepper.

Combine Bread and Custard:
- Pour the custard mixture over the bread cubes. Gently toss to ensure that all the bread cubes are coated in the mixture.

Let Soak:
- Allow the bread to soak in the custard mixture for about 15-20 minutes, ensuring that the bread absorbs the liquid.

Transfer to Baking Dish:
- Transfer the bread and custard mixture to a greased baking dish, spreading it evenly.

Top with Parmesan:
- Sprinkle additional Parmesan cheese on top of the bread pudding.

Bake:
- Bake in the preheated oven for 35-40 minutes or until the top is golden brown, and the pudding is set.

Garnish and Serve:
- Remove from the oven, garnish with chopped fresh parsley, and let it cool for a few minutes before serving.

Serve Warm:
- Serve the Garlic Parmesan Bread Pudding warm as a side dish or a delicious savory main course.

This flavorful bread pudding is a great accompaniment to a variety of dishes or can be enjoyed on its own. Enjoy!

Buffalo Chicken Dip

Ingredients:

- 2 cups shredded cooked chicken (rotisserie chicken works well)
- 8 oz (about 1 cup) cream cheese, softened
- 1/2 cup ranch dressing
- 1/2 cup buffalo sauce
- 1 cup shredded cheddar cheese
- 1/2 cup crumbled blue cheese (optional)
- 1/4 cup green onions, chopped (for garnish)
- Tortilla chips, celery sticks, or carrot sticks (for serving)

Instructions:

Preheat Oven:
- Preheat your oven to 350°F (175°C).

Prepare Chicken:
- Shred the cooked chicken into small, bite-sized pieces.

Mix Ingredients:
- In a mixing bowl, combine the shredded chicken, softened cream cheese, ranch dressing, buffalo sauce, shredded cheddar cheese, and crumbled blue cheese (if using). Mix until well combined.

Transfer to Baking Dish:
- Transfer the mixture to a greased baking dish, spreading it evenly.

Bake:
- Bake in the preheated oven for about 25-30 minutes, or until the dip is hot and bubbly, and the top is lightly browned.

Garnish:
- Remove from the oven and garnish with chopped green onions.

Serve:
- Serve the Buffalo Chicken Dip warm with tortilla chips, celery sticks, or carrot sticks for dipping.

This Buffalo Chicken Dip is perfect for game days, parties, or any gathering where you want to enjoy a delicious and spicy appetizer. Enjoy!

Slow Cooker Cornbread

Ingredients:

- 1 cup cornmeal
- 1 cup all-purpose flour
- 1 tablespoon baking powder
- 1/2 teaspoon baking soda
- 1/2 teaspoon salt
- 2 large eggs
- 1 cup buttermilk
- 1/4 cup unsalted butter, melted
- 1/4 cup honey or sugar (optional, for sweetness)
- Cooking spray or butter (for greasing the slow cooker)

Instructions:

Grease Slow Cooker:
- Grease the inside of your slow cooker with cooking spray or butter to prevent sticking.

Mix Dry Ingredients:
- In a mixing bowl, whisk together the cornmeal, all-purpose flour, baking powder, baking soda, and salt.

Mix Wet Ingredients:
- In another bowl, whisk the eggs and then add buttermilk, melted butter, and honey or sugar (if using). Mix well.

Combine Mixtures:
- Pour the wet ingredients into the dry ingredients. Stir until just combined. Do not overmix; it's okay if there are a few lumps.

Transfer to Slow Cooker:
- Pour the cornbread batter into the greased slow cooker, spreading it evenly.

Cook on Low:
- Cover the slow cooker and cook on low for 2 to 3 hours, or until a toothpick inserted into the center comes out clean.

Check for Doneness:
- Around the 2-hour mark, start checking for doneness by inserting a toothpick into the center of the cornbread. If it comes out clean or with a few crumbs (not wet batter), it's done.

Cool and Slice:
- Once cooked, let the cornbread cool in the slow cooker for a bit before slicing.

Serve:
- Serve the Slow Cooker Cornbread as a side dish with butter, honey, or your favorite topping.

This slow cooker cornbread is moist, flavorful, and a great addition to your meal. Enjoy!

Jalapeño Popper Dip

Ingredients:

- 8 oz cream cheese, softened
- 1 cup mayonnaise
- 1 cup shredded cheddar cheese
- 1 cup shredded Monterey Jack cheese
- 1/2 cup grated Parmesan cheese
- 6-8 jalapeños, seeds removed and finely chopped
- 1 cup breadcrumbs
- 1/2 cup grated Parmesan cheese (for topping)
- 1/4 cup chopped green onions (for garnish, optional)
- Tortilla chips or sliced baguette (for serving)

Instructions:

Preheat Oven:
- Preheat your oven to 375°F (190°C).

Mix Cream Cheese and Mayonnaise:
- In a mixing bowl, combine softened cream cheese and mayonnaise. Mix until smooth and well combined.

Add Cheeses and Jalapeños:
- Add shredded cheddar, shredded Monterey Jack, grated Parmesan, and finely chopped jalapeños to the cream cheese mixture. Stir until the cheeses and jalapeños are evenly distributed.

Transfer to Baking Dish:
- Transfer the mixture to a greased baking dish, spreading it evenly.

Prepare Topping:
- In a small bowl, combine breadcrumbs and additional grated Parmesan cheese for the topping.

Top with Breadcrumbs:
- Sprinkle the breadcrumb and Parmesan mixture evenly over the jalapeño popper dip.

Bake:
- Bake in the preheated oven for about 25-30 minutes or until the top is golden brown and the dip is bubbly.

Garnish and Serve:

- Remove from the oven, garnish with chopped green onions if desired, and let it cool for a few minutes before serving.

Serve Warm:
- Serve the Jalapeño Popper Dip warm with tortilla chips or sliced baguette.

This dip is perfect for spice lovers and makes a great addition to party platters or game day spreads. Enjoy the creamy and spicy goodness!

Slow Cooker Rosemary Garlic Potatoes

Ingredients:

- 2.5 lbs (about 1.1 kg) baby potatoes, halved or quartered
- 3 tablespoons olive oil
- 4 cloves garlic, minced
- 1 tablespoon fresh rosemary, chopped
- Salt and black pepper to taste
- Optional: 1/4 cup grated Parmesan cheese (for garnish)
- Fresh parsley, chopped (for garnish)

Instructions:

Prepare Potatoes:
- Wash and cut the baby potatoes into halves or quarters, depending on their size.

Combine Ingredients:
- In a bowl, mix the halved or quartered potatoes with olive oil, minced garlic, chopped rosemary, salt, and black pepper. Toss until the potatoes are well coated.

Transfer to Slow Cooker:
- Transfer the seasoned potatoes to the slow cooker, spreading them evenly.

Cook on Low:
- Cover the slow cooker and cook on low for 4-5 hours or until the potatoes are tender. The cooking time may vary based on your slow cooker.

Optional Parmesan Garnish:
- If desired, sprinkle grated Parmesan cheese over the cooked potatoes during the last 30 minutes of cooking.

Check for Seasoning:
- Taste and adjust the seasoning if necessary.

Garnish and Serve:
- Before serving, garnish the Slow Cooker Rosemary Garlic Potatoes with fresh chopped parsley.

Serve Warm:
- Serve the potatoes warm as a side dish with your favorite main course.

These slow-cooked potatoes infused with rosemary and garlic make for a delicious and aromatic side dish. Enjoy!